CAN YOU HEAR ME ?

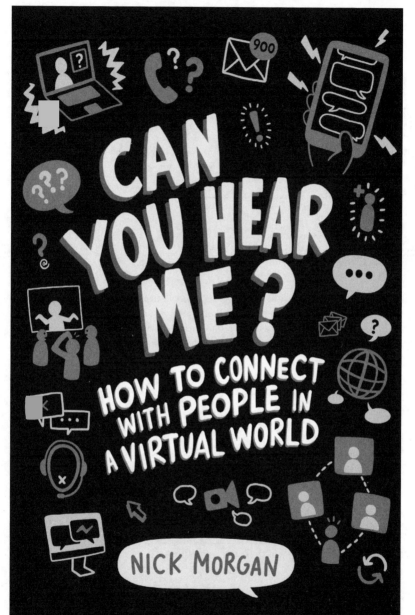

CAN YOU HEAR ME?

HOW TO CONNECT WITH PEOPLE IN A VIRTUAL WORLD

NICK MORGAN

Harvard Business Review Press

Boston, Massachusetts

Library of Congress Cataloging-in-Publication Data

Names: Morgan, Nick, author.
Title: Can you hear me? : how to connect with people in a virtual world / Nick Morgan.
Description: Boston, Massachusetts : Harvard Business Review Press, [2018] | Includes bibliographical references and index.
Identifiers: LCCN 2018037883 | ISBN 9781633694446 (hardcover : alk. paper)
Subjects: LCSH: Communication and technology. | Business communication. | Teleconferencing. | Communication—Psychological aspects.
Classification: LCC P96.T42 M665 2018 | DDC 302.23/1—dc23
LC record available at https://lccn.loc.gov/2018037883

ISBN: 978-1-63369-444-6
eISBN: 978-1-63369-445-3

The paper used in this publication meets the requirements of the American National Standard for Permanence of Paper for Publications and Documents in Libraries and Archives Z39.48-1992.

To Nikki, the center of my world

To Sarah, Eric, Howard, and Emma, bridging old worlds and new

To Lakin, Logan, Eryn, Thaila, and Cyril, knowing only the new

CONTENTS

PART TWO

SPECIFIC TECHNIQUES FOR SPECIFIC DIGITAL CHANNELS

PROLOGUE
IS THIS THING ON?

We are all unwitting participants in a massive social experiment that began slowly after World War II and gathered speed in the last decade with the introduction of the smartphone. We have created virtual personas, online worlds, digital connections, social media lives, email relationships, audioconference teams—the whole panoply of ways that we now communicate with one another virtually.

That ability to communicate virtually seemed at first to be an unmitigated advance. We could communicate faster, more easily, with less friction, at our own convenience, to multiples of our previous audiences, with the click of a mouse or a "send" button.

Only recently have we started to realize that this huge social experiment has a downside, too. We've started to worry about shorter attention spans, and we wonder if the internet makes us stupid. But the real downside has remained largely invisible to us because it touches on the workings of our unconscious minds.

As we've made room for virtual communication in our lives, our workplaces, and in all the ways we connect with one another, we haven't fully realized how emotionally empty virtual communications are. Every form of virtual communication strips out the emotional subtext of our communications to a greater or lesser extent. Every one.

Take email, for example. We've all experienced the frustration of sending an email that was (to us) obviously meant to be a joke. But the recipient, instead of being amused, was offended, and we had to spend huge amounts of time repairing the relationship. That's the simplest, most obvious form of emotional undercutting that virtual communications foist on us.

Most of us have also spent hours on audioconferences at work, with the mute button in force, taking care of other business while people on the other end of the box drone on endlessly. We've had to lunge for that mute button when the boss suddenly says, "Nick, are you still on? What do you think of the new cross-eyed widget?"

And then there's social media, which would seem to be all about emotional connection but in fact is like Pringles potato chips; you need to keep eating them because one chip doesn't satisfy. The bland taste creates a need for more but doesn't allow you to stop. We get one like on Facebook, enjoy a brief hit of pleasure, and crave more. We get social love on Twitter and Instagram, and it's just enough to keep us checking our mobile phones hundreds of times per day. In short, we've transferred a surprisingly large amount of our human interactions to the virtual world, and as a result, we no longer get the emotional information, support, and reinforcement we used to get without thinking about it while communicating face-to-face.

Virtual relationships are more fragile and easily disrupted because they lack the unconscious connections our face-to-face interactions automatically convey. The lift of an eyebrow, the tone of a voice, a quick smile, a shake of the head—these are the ways we decode other people's intents. These signals are largely absent from all forms of digital communication.

In business, this absence leads to miscommunication, misunderstandings, and a huge amount of do-overs, workarounds, and relationship repair. It's expensive. It's inefficient. And the cost in fractured relationships, missed opportunities, and lost connections is incalculable. Because we make decisions with our emotions, moreover, when we take them out of the communication, the audioconference, or the webinar, it becomes almost impossible to make good decisions when we're immersed in the virtual stream.

In our personal lives, the same problems occur, especially when we're trying to connect with someone at a distance, virtually. It's expensive in many less quantifiable ways.

The result of this massive social experiment is a huge increase in loneliness, social isolation, fear of missing out (FOMO), and Instagram/Facebook envy, and, tragically, teenage depression and even suicide. We may be raising a generation of people who are unhappy communicating virtually and incompetent communicating face-to-face. Those of us with one foot in the face-to-face world and one foot in the virtual world are torn. We are invested in both, but we lack the time to master either world or feel completely at home in both.

What's to be done? The experiment will continue. We can't live without our gadgets. Too much of our personal and work lives today relies on the virtual. Indeed, most organizations with an international reach couldn't function without the digital means of communication they use every day.

But we need to learn to live smarter and communicate differently to survive in this brave new digital world. We need to begin to consciously add the emotional subtext back into our virtual communications to avoid the costs—personal and financial—associated with miscommunication.

That's the subject of this book.

CAN YOU HEAR ME ?

INTRODUCTION

WE'RE MORE CONNECTED THAN EVER, SO WHY DO I FEEL SO ALONE?

"It's state of the art." I was being ushered into half a conference room in Boston. The other half was in Denmark, at another branch office of the company I was consulting with. My assignment was to coach a half-dozen executives preparing for an important meeting at which they would all be speaking. These executives were spread around the world, some in the United States, some in Europe, and some in Asia.

This day, I was coaching one executive. She wouldn't be back in the United States for a week or two, and it was important that she start rehearsing sooner than that. The solution was to put her in one-half of a conference room that showed up virtually in the US office where I was seated.

"It's as good as being in the same room," was the considered opinion of her administrative assistant, who was leading me into the windowless room that promised to deliver Denmark to me. "It's state of the art."

I sat down, as instructed, in a chair in front of a curved table that looked like part of an expensive business school auditorium.

In front of me, instead of a stage and lectern, was a screen. On the screen was the mirror image of the room I was in—the same curved table, with chairs, and microphones in front of each chair.

It was like looking into a huge mirror. Only the half of the room inside the mirror was empty.

I glanced around the room and waited. The assistant whispered a few instructions. "Speak into the microphone. It's voice activated. Tap it. Don't stand up. And you don't have to shout."

I wondered why she had told me not to stand. She left. In a minute or two, in walked the torso of what I presumed was my executive.

Her head was cut off. I learned later that "state of the art" only allowed for a picture that covered people sitting in chairs. People of average height. Very tall people had to slump slightly in their chairs.

When she sat down, I could see her face.

"— you?" she said.

After a moment's confusion, I realized that she must have asked me how I was. The voice-activated microphone had cut off the first words of her response.

I tapped the microphone and said, "(*tap*) I'm fine, thanks. How are you?"

The coaching conversation proceeded in a strange series of percussive sounds and overlapping comments. By the end of the session, we were shouting at each other. I wasn't sure why. We could see each other well enough unless we stood up. We could hear each other, as long as we kept tapping the mic before speaking. Why did it feel like such hard work, and why did we end up shouting at each other? Why was an hour or two all we could sustain? What was so hard about something that looked almost like we were in the same room? (I'll answer those immediate questions at the end of this introduction and take up a more in-depth discussion of the problems and opportunities of video-conferencing in chapter 9.)

For most people, moving into the digital world to communicate means experiencing significant loss of clarity, ease, and depth. You struggle to convey the lightness of tone you want in an email, and you risk offending your colleague because the smile doesn't come through. You tune out during an audioconference because some connection is missing and you can't stay focused virtually for ninety minutes. You flounder to find the right sense of engagement on a Skype call. It's a job interview, but the interviewer is calling in from her home office (as you are), and how does that change the dynamics of the interview? Are you at home or at work? Is the right tone more or less open, more or less formal, more or less sincere?

You can't find good emotional footing in the virtual world today

Over and over again, people find that they struggle when trying to communicate virtually. Something—a lot—is missing. It's harder to get the nuances, the emotions, and the details right. Does that mean that the digital world makes us stupider? Less able to concentrate? Less desirous of an emotional connection?

No, but it demands that we learn to behave differently. We need to learn a new set of rules—like learning to communicate in a new language. The virtual pushes us to invest in multiple different worlds, often simultaneously. These new worlds come with new, vague codes of conduct and create new needs. A lot of work we used to take for granted, because it was done automatically by our unconscious minds in face-to-face communications, now has to be done consciously and intentionally. The digital world forces us to rewire our unconscious communication habits for conscious success.

And clearly, we urgently need to learn to avoid the traps of the digital world and its new forms of communications. For example, psychologists have identified a new phobia: nomophobia, the fear of trying to live without your cell phone.[1] And yet, much research shows that as our digital engagement goes up, our personal sense of loneliness increases just as fast.[2] Why this perverse attachment to tools that are actually increasing our sense of detachment? We develop Facebook FOMO, Twitter envy, and LinkedIn loss. And we respond by diving more deeply into the very digital means of our discontent. The virtual water we drink simply makes us thirstier.

We're more connected than ever, and more alone

We need help.

In-person communication is incredibly rich, loaded with information about how the person we're talking to is feeling at every second of the conversation. It's satisfying in a way that virtual communication can't be. Virtual communication is much flatter—online conversation requires us to deliberately engage our own and other people's emotions.

We need a new rule book for conscious communication in the digital age. Our unconscious minds fail us at the doorway to the digital world. We have to learn how to put as much of the missing emotion, pattern recognition, and memory back into the digital world that those well-intentioned engineers have stripped out.

That's what the book you're holding in your hands (or reading on a Kindle, or listening to with earbuds, or having directly implanted into your brain by some technology waiting to be invented) will show you how to do. This book offers a Fodor's guide for the unknown digital country we find ourselves in, because how can we leave it? We need the digital realm, and yet the cost of living in it is far too high, psychologically speaking.

The opportunity cost of free, fast information is surprisingly high

Now you know the grim truth about this brave new digital world. What specific problems does it raise for us inhabitants of the world of work—those of us who have to get stuff done? And what can we do to make things better? The rest of this chapter will sketch out the main ideas this book covers on the digital-communications conundrum.

Sadly, the more we learn, the worse this world we've created looks. Study after study documents the impoverishing effect of life in the digital era: the absurd collation of unlimited data, supercomputers in our pockets, and endlessly trite, recycled, bite-sized information fed to us in ways that make sense for machines to broadcast but not for humans to receive.[3]

And even worse, although we can't easily see how the digital world makes some work harder, the difficulty is no less crippling. Let's take a quick tour of the research on what happens to good communicators in the virtual world.

With email, recipients are less cooperative—and feel more justified in not cooperating.[4] They feel more entitled to lie.[5] They evaluate each other more harshly because of reduced feelings of social obligation.[6] It turns out, for example, that if you have even a brief conversation over the phone before trying to negotiate via email, it goes better.[7] Or, if you use a webcam to make eye contact with someone you're about to debate with, the conversation goes better, with less hostility.[8] Eye contact enables us to determine, in the long run, who's dominant and, in the short run, who's talking.[9] In general, workplaces that make an effort to put back in the workplace some of the absent human emotions—the emotions so easily conveyed in face-to-face conversations, the "I care" kind of feelings—reduce absenteeism and burnout and increase employee engagement.[10]

Virtual communication sabotages us in unexpected ways

People who use social words in their communications, words like *coffee* or *football*, are less likely to get fired.[11]

By now, you won't be surprised to learn that no one except you pays attention on conference calls.[12] Of course you do. Those hilarious anecdotes you've heard about people doing silly, random, and disgusting things while muted on a conference call? They're doing those things because they're completely disengaged from that important call you scheduled for Monday morning to kick the week off right at each of your crucial centers around the globe.

True confession: I started casting—if that's the right word—tarot cards while on innumerable conference calls. And I'm not a believer. Just to pass the time. Until I discovered pacing and lifting free weights. Now I'm trying to get in shape while half-listening to all those calls.

Strangely, doodling helps you pay attention.[13] Maybe that's because doodling engages your unconscious mind.

Maybe you should doodle while texting. Researchers recently found that the more you rely on texting to sustain your romantic relationships, the less satisfying those relationships are.[14] But don't be texting while in a meeting—three-quarters of your coworkers find it annoying, no matter how cleverly you try to disguise what you're doing.[15] We can tell.

Of course, people think they communicate more clearly over email than they actually do.[16] Tone is very hard to communicate; there's emotion rearing its pesky head again. As John Medina, a molecular biologist with a PhD and the author of *Brain Rules*, notes, we don't pay attention to boring things. Vision trumps the other senses. But even video calls are sensory-poor experiences compared with face-to-face encounters, because of the air pressure, the smells, the ambient sound in the room. All the sensory input of all five senses and a few more that we're only just beginning to learn about are condensed or eliminated on video.[17]

We were meant to communicate face-to-face, outdoors, in constant motion

As Medina says, "the human brain appears to have been designed to solve problems related to surviving in an outdoor setting, in unstable meteorological conditions, and to do so in near-constant motion." That's what fully engages our senses and our unconscious minds. None of those conditions are usually present or optimal in the digital world. And, he continues, people "ought to really understand that the brain processes meaning before it processes detail. It wants the meaning of what it is that you're talking about before it wants the detail of what it is you're talking about."[18] In other words, we want to know why first and then how or what.

According to neuroscientists, when the brain encounters something new, which is a good deal of our waking life, it starts to ask questions. It immediately queries the inputs it receives from the outside world with six essential concerns—all to do, not surprisingly, with survival. Will it eat me? Can I eat it? Can I have sex with it? Can it have sex with me? Have I seen it before? Have I never seen it before? Can you imagine how the third-quarter financial numbers compete on a conference call with those other questions running around subconsciously in the participants' minds?

Finally, the unconscious mind craves the big picture—the sort of overview you might have gotten in caveperson days from an outcropping a hundred yards above the savanna—and, at the same time, refuge. The safety of the cave. The virtual world, by putting us into our heads, gives us neither overview nor refuge.[19]

Virtual communication engenders five big problems seldom encountered in person

The first big problem with virtual communication is the lack of feedback. This is the problem from which all the rest of the problems in the virtual world flow. Humans (in an evolutionary sense) are relatively feeble creatures. We run the risk of falling victim to lots of bigger animals with paws and teeth that can reduce us to dinner with a swipe or a bite. So, we evolved to be prediction junkies and became adept at scouting out patterns. We want to know, always, what's going to happen next, and we want to know, does that shadow mean a tiger is lurking over there?

Our brains constantly scan the spaces around us, looking for danger patterns and making predictions. We use the five senses that we're aware of, and others that only our unconscious minds keep track of, like sensing the way the air changes around us when other humans or animals are drawing near.

The virtual world usually deprives us of most of those sources of sensory information. We simply don't get the feedback we're used to getting constantly and analyzing continuously. Our brains respond by filling up the sensory data with memories, made-up stuff, and anxiety. And thus we find the virtual world repetitive, confusing, and tension-filled. We suffer in the virtual world primarily because of the lack of sensory feedback.

The second big problem is related to the first: the lack of empathy. Because we get little information in virtual communication, we learn little about how other people are feeling. The mirror neurons that normally send us constant data about other people's emotions are deprived of the sensory feed, and so they once again make it up. You start to imagine that the person on the other end of that email is angry at you, because you don't really know what the person is thinking.

This lack of information, and the resulting misinformation filling the pipeline, lead us to poor or incorrect analyses of other people's emotional states. Our normal high levels of empathy are reduced or rendered inaccurate.

A side issue of the lack of empathy is that the virtual world is less interesting, since a big part of what engages our time and attention in the real world is figuring out what other people are feeling. And so, in the virtual world, attention spans are shorter, maybe as short as ten minutes.[20] But habit dictates that meetings are usually scheduled in hour-long segments, some even longer. Our meetings, especially virtual ones, are outstripping our attention spans.

The third big problem is the lack of control over your own persona. This problem develops in the virtual emotional desert. Because the virtual world is arranged largely by and for machines, it can remember everything. This capacity means that you leave endless digital footprints everywhere you go. In the real world, people forget and forgive. In the virtual world, as many job applicants have found, all those embarrassing photos from your wild college parties are still out there, ripe for the harvesting.

As we'll see, you can manage your virtual persona to a certain extent, but on the whole, it's as if every step you ever took were memorialized in wet cement as you ventured forth. The virtual world is the wet cement for every digital step you take.

The fourth big problem is the lack of emotion. The human mind is constantly assessing its surroundings and the intent of all the people within its ken. Take away the emotional subtext, and an odd thing happens: we have a hard time making decisions. Most of us believe we made decisions as Mr. Spock did. That is, we think consciously and logically and make decisions accordingly. But a good deal of neuroscience has clearly established that we make decisions in our unconscious minds, basing them on memories and on emotions.[21] As a result, our ability to decide things in the virtual world is severely constricted. We have a hard time deciding, we make faulty decisions on scanty or misinterpreted data, and we end up tuning out altogether.

For example, we've all experienced the mess we can make with one misinterpreted email, where somebody imagines a tone that we didn't intend. The same thing can happen in an audioconference. Does the silence in response to what you've just said mean that everyone is in rapt agreement or that everyone is tuned out—or that people are on mute so that they can have a party? You don't know, you can't decide, and it's all too much hard work.

And the last big problem is the lack of connection—and commitment. Humans crave connection, and the virtual world seems endlessly social. But real connection, like decision making, is based on emotions. Take the emotions out, and we feel alone more often than makes sense. The bonding that naturally happens when people meet face-to-face and size each other up, fall in love, find mutual interests, and so on, is lacking. And thus with thousands of Twitter followers, oodles of Instagram and

Facebook friends, and a huge LinkedIn community, we're still left endlessly chasing the junk food of connection online—likes, clicks, and links that give us a passing thrill but no real sense of connection like a hug.

As a result, a formidable issue for us humans is that online commitment—trust—is fragile. Trolling (nasty, unproductive baiting and name-calling) is rampant. The whole emotional life of the online world is, in short, a train wreck for the way the human mind actually works.

I'll address these five problems in more detail in the next five chapters and then offer some commonsense solutions in the concluding chapters, which look at various methods of virtual communication. First, a couple of caveats. These five problems overlap, of course. Because they concern human psychology, they're messy and not cleanly divided. The lack of feedback and the resultant decrease in empathy; the loss of control over virtual information; diminished emotion, which hurts decision making; and the fragile commitments and trust from a lack of connection are all, well, interconnected. But they are distinct and important enough to warrant separate discussions in subsequent chapters.

And finally, we are in the early days of research. Writing this book, I was constantly encountering new studies that might affect what I would say. I've been frustrated by the lack of strong research in other areas. We have thousands more questions than answers about virtual communications. And I've been struck by how one study may undercut another because there is no definitive position on a particular issue. Our present knowledge about the brain and communications may not be what we know later. Indeed, one neuroscientist said to me in an off-the-record comment as I was conducting the interview, "We know nothing about the brain."

Of course, he meant "nothing for certain," yet his observation is a healthy reminder to proceed with caution. But that doesn't mean that we can't make some essential, enduring observations about the main—and glaring—problems with virtual communications and begin to suggest what to do about them.

———————

Now back to that videoconference. Why did it feel like such hard work? A brief analysis of how face-to-face communication works will help answer those questions I asked at the beginning. If you want to get right to the five problems, then this would be a good time to jump to chapter 1.

Emotional truth is as important in communications as intellectual truth

We humans learned to communicate when we dressed in skins, fought with clubs, and talked in grunts. The human community was a frail group arrayed against monsters like woolly mammoths and saber-toothed cats. Speed of reaction was essential. Instant reading of intent—correctly—meant the difference between life and death. We learned to communicate quickly, unconsciously, and simply.

We based our reactions on what we learned about humans and other animals, recognizing patterns and acting on them instantly to keep on living. To keep those patterns—and memories of those patterns—fresh, we ordered them in a hierarchy of importance determined by emotional tags. The most frightening things we remembered best. Every day, our brains learned to scrub away the less emotional memories to start again, retaining the patterns and memories that seemed the most important—the most scary, closely followed by relevance to food, shelter, sex, and the other essentials.

That was 300,000 years ago. Things didn't change much for roughly 299,900 years. Then humans started communicating virtually. As we'll explore in more depth in the following pages, virtual communications unintentionally stripped out most of the emotional structure of face-to-face communications, while making it much easier to connect with more people faster and with less effort.

The result? We were soon both overwhelmed and bored.

When humans communicate face-to-face, we do so with little conscious effort most of the time. Even when language is a barrier, we can quickly get the gist of the idea through body language, facial expression, and the emotion conveyed. When we communicate at a distance, the effort involved is considerable and the opportunities for miscommunication are multiplied.

Face-to-face communication is the norm for human behavior, even though it is getting hard to remember ever living life without a mobile phone. We evolved over millennia to communicate quickly, efficiently, and easily face-to-face. What happens when you put that fabulous organic communicating machine to work in a virtual environment?

The virtual environment is disastrous for our normal modes of communicating

Picture a worker in a cubicle. Gray walls, gray chair, gray computer. Gray hum of background noise all around. When she picks up the phone, the way the voice is processed over that instrument cuts out most of the emotion. That's why telephone calls and webinars are so boring. No emotion.

Now stretch that picture out, day after day, month after month, year after year. Is it any wonder that 70 percent of your workers are either actively disengaged or not engaged, according to the last Gallup poll?[22] Another recent study found that regular face-to-face communication cuts the risk of depression in adults by half. Phone and email don't have the same effect.[23]

Our unconscious minds need to get together so that they can find the emotional connections they crave. We humans are social beings. We don't do well when deprived of our fellow humans. We need to feed that unconscious mind, and we starve it at our peril as employers, as employees, as humans. We need face-to-face.

The virtual world is impoverished for us humans. We haven't had time—evolutionary time—to change to accommodate the communication shift of the past half century.

We are lost, bored, and alone.

Let's go a little deeper. What are some of the most important missing pieces? Think about how a normal face-to-face conversation goes. You use eye contact at the beginning to make sure you've got the other person's attention, and then you launch into that story about the drunk dog. You start looking up, down, and sideways for inspiration, to recall the tale, and simply to give your listener a break. Then, when you're ready to wrap up and hand the conversational baton off to your partner, you check back in with the person with a clear signal of eye contact to say, "Almost done. Get ready."

Without eye contact, we have a hard time talking

Eye contact is thus an important regulator of communication. And it's almost entirely missing from the virtual world.

What other areas of communication are important to face-to-face conversations—and what are the perils in the virtual world? Let's start with email, since that's where the digital world really took off. The digital era began, arguably, with email and the attempt to solve two particular problems with older forms of communication: time and money. Letters, memos, and other forms of written communication, such as reports and white papers, were full of what the Silicon Valley calls *friction*—they were hard to create and cost money. And face-to-face communications required that busy schedules be synchronized. The engineers and scientists at Massachusetts Institute of Technology (MIT) and in the defense industry wanted communication that was both frictionless and asynchronous.

The first email proper was sent in 1971 over something called ARPANET as a way for university researchers and defense contractors to share information that met the two criteria. Both problems were solved, and the digital era began. Communication became frictionless and asynchronous, and Pandora's digital box had opened.

Why did these laudable efforts eventually produce an emotional train wreck for the rest of us? In solving the problems of time and money, digital communication unintentionally created two other problems: we gradually became awash in email, and most of it was boring. But there lurked a deeper problem that only became apparent once we were firmly ensconced in the digital era (and the thrill of new technology had worn off): the emotional components of the letter (or even the telegraph) were stripped away. In exchange for asynchronous, frictionless communication, we got information overload and the emotional banality of the always-on social media era.

But it gets worse.

The main work of our minds is unconscious

Our minds are driven mostly by unconscious processes.[24] We get an unconscious thought or desire. We make an unconscious decision. Then our bodies act on that decision, and only after that do our conscious minds catch up, notice what's going on, and take credit for what just happened. The mind edits out any awareness of the lag between unconscious impulse and conscious thought, presumably so we won't have to experience the vertigo of finding our bodies acting without our prior conscious knowledge.

That unconscious mind can analyze something like eleven million bits of information per second, while our conscious minds can only process about forty.[25] The unconscious mind has thus taken over most of our thought processes to keep us alive and safe. We react with our bodies milliseconds before our minds would even notice danger, saved by the split-second, lifesaving decisions of the unconscious. Like former president George W. Bush, who famously dodged an errant shoe thrown at him by a disgruntled Iraqi reporter at a news conference in the Green Zone, we move before we think. And that's a good thing.

But we also decide before we think, consciously, and that's a bit more problematic. We rely on our emotional memories and unconscious memory patterns to make decisions. Avoid strawberries; they make you sick! Find another way home; this feels dangerous! She's just not that into you!

Why is our tendency to decide on an unconscious level a problem, and what does it have to do with email? When you talk to someone face-to-face, you automatically absorb the emotional state of the person in front of you. Especially if you know someone well, you know whether the person is serious when he or she says, "Your hair is on fire," or is just kidding. That knowledge enables you to decide how to hear and understand the communication you're receiving. It's based on the emotion-tagged memories you have of your previous interaction with that person and a whole host of other interactions and memories.

Most of us simply don't appreciate that our decisions, our nego-tiations with other human beings, and our daily analysis of the familiar and the strange are expedited by two well-oiled uncon-scious processes: recognizing patterns and attaching meaning to them through emotion. Imagine the young child putting the proverbial finger on the hot stove. Instantly, the child's uncon-scious mind is seething with shock, anger, pain, bafflement. The little one is never going to do that again. Pattern recognition and emotional-memory tagging will ensure that he or she never even comes close.

That's how our minds work. Take away the emotion, and we can't get purchase on that mountain of messaging. You send and receive messages through email, and suddenly you and your recipients lack those immediate cues and your emotional-memory decision systems aren't triggered. You either find the messages simply boring or interpret them incorrectly. Either way, you're wrong.

Add to that a huge increase in the number of messages com-ing at you, because email is so easy to send, and suddenly, your whole decision-making process is registering overload. You can't keep up, and you can't decide the relative importance of all the stuff coming at you. Triage is hard to do, and most of the information is deeply uninteresting, anyway. When you do react strongly to something, your reaction may be just as likely a misreading as a correct interpretation.

And so, in sum, email (and texting, and Slack, and all the other forms of text-based communication) is frictionless and asynchronous. But it's also boring, overwhelming, and difficult to deal with. That's the real state of the digital era.

In contrast, face-to-face communications, the kind we evolved to handle very, very well, are fast, data-rich, and mostly unconscious.

The digital era is a communications disaster

I've focused on email so far to make things clear. But the same problem bedevils all the digital era's attempts to replace inefficient face-to-face talk with more efficient ways to transcend time and place—and make it easy. The engineers and scientists who launched the digital era weren't particularly aware of, and thus weren't thinking about, the virtues of face-to-face communications. As a result, they didn't optimize the various kinds of digital communications for what humans need: data-rich, emotionally complex, fast exchanges of human intent and meaning, largely through the unconscious mind.

Like most of us, maybe more so because they were engineers, they were only aware of their conscious minds. By definition, the unconscious remains just that, hidden away from the ego-saturated, confident, logical-seeming conscious mind. The latter thinks it's in charge, like the Western child who thinks that milk comes in a carton, meat in a plastic-wrapped package, and entertainment everywhere on devices you can pinch and swipe to your heart's content. Accordingly, the engineers gave us email, telephones and voice mail, video calls, and various other combinations of these digital sounds and images—most of which had the emotional components unintentionally engineered out of them.

Let's take the phone as a further, and important, example. When engineers were figuring out ways to condense the signal that is the human voice, they noticed that those voices were made up of three bands of sound. There's the pitch people speak at, which at the low end (mostly men) goes as low as 85 hertz and at the high end (mostly women) goes as high as 255 hertz. That's a narrow range, when you consider that if you have good ears, you can hear from 20 to 20,000 hertz. The engineers figured they could get the important part of human speech if they just took the 85- to 255-hertz range and cut out the overtones and undertones of human voices; these tones range considerably above and below the range of audible pitch.

What are the undertones and overtones? You don't hear them consciously, but, unconsciously, you're incredibly good at picking them up. Every human voice has a slightly different mix of pitch, undertones, and overtones. Added together, these features give each voice a distinctive quality—what musicians call the timbre of an instrument, only for the voice. You are so good at hearing the timbre of human voices that you can identify every human voice you know—typically hundreds—in an instant, without being aware that you're doing any work and without consciously hearing the undertones and overtones. You just blur them all together in John's voice or Jane's voice.

Your unconscious mind has amazing power

The ability to distinguish hundreds of people by voice is an astonishing feat when you think about it. It's the unconscious at work again, running mental circles around the conscious mind, teeing up voices, patterns, and memories at unbelievable speeds, all before the conscious mind even knows something is about to happen. Milliseconds before, for the most part, but still well before your consciousness catches on, and in time for most predicaments.

Because the engineers working on telephones cut out most of those undertones and overtones, voices don't sound quite as distinctive on the phone but are still distinctive enough to be told apart, usually, by the unconscious. So far, so bad.

But here's where it gets really interesting. It turns out that the emotions in human voices are carried by the undertones, so that when you cut out some of that spectrum of sound, you take the emotion out of voices. It's why audioconferences are so boring. And when you realize that you base some decisions on your emotions, you begin to see that audioconferences, internet calls, most computerized phone systems, and most computer video systems based on the same bandwidth compression are all rendered both uninteresting and difficult to think about usefully. Sure, you register boredom, but is that the best basis from which to make your decisions?

What's more, we pick leaders according to the authority in their undertones. When US presidential candidates Barack Obama and John McCain debated, McCain was generally considered to have won the first two debates. And when researchers analyzed the men's vocal patterns, lo and behold, they found that Obama had matched his undertones to McCain's—thus showing that Obama, at least, was deferring to McCain. The voters thought so too, and McCain was ahead in the polls.[26]

In the third debate, roughly one week after the second, Obama suddenly took command. McCain matched his own undertone vocal patterns to Obama's, and Obama was widely considered to have won this debate. He took the lead in the polls and won the presidency.

We pick our leaders in a surprising way

Leadership is determined by the vocal patterns of our undertones, most of which are usually removed from digital audio communications. In other words, you can't lead a team effectively over the phone or any other similar digital means. And it's harder to pay attention, make decisions, analyze meaning, recognize patterns, and have those deep aha moments—all the mental work everyone counts on in the information age. And yet the chance are good, if you're reading this book, that this is exactly what you're trying to do.

What about video; does adding a visual element help? And the answer is yes, of course, video helps somewhat. But it brings its own challenges. Why do most people find video such hard work? Why do people tend to shout during videoconferences even when others tell the shouters they can hear just fine?

Your unconscious mind manages yet another incredible feat while you're talking face-to-face with someone else. We tend to move closer to people, ideas, and things we like and away from those we don't like. It's a body-language signal that most people are not very good at disguising. We rear back our heads, for example, when we are hit with an offensive smell, person, or idea.

Now, your unconscious not only notices visually that the people around you are moving back and forth as a gauge of their moods, but it also notices the small changes in the air caused by those motions. When you're watching someone on a video-conference, your unconscious mind is looking for those breezy clues, but when it receives no such clues, it decides that the other person is further away than he or she actually is.

We cannot easily measure the distance between us online

Hence the shouting. And why people feel that video calls are hard work. Video calls are to face-to-face communications as tin-can telephones are to real phones. (And remember that phones are hard work, too.)

Much of the digital world is effectively two-dimensional, when our minds crave three-dimensional. The audio stream is reduced. The emotions are blocked or deracinated. Video is in fact two-dimensional and lacks essential sensory input. Email and text lack tonal and audible clues to intent. In system after system, the bandwidth is reduced in imperceptible ways that relate to emotion and the core human-thinking processes.

And the flatness of digital is also partly why we find digital communications such hard work. They feel as if they should be easy. And being mostly frictionless, they are easier in some ways. But in unconscious ways that we can't easily appreciate, they are sorely lacking, and we find it hard to compensate as a result.

We humans crave connection with other humans

In the end, we humans are a social, empathetic species, and we crave the basic connection that comes from urgent, authentic, face-to-face communications. We're wired to live in that world.

When humans communicate face-to-face, they exchange huge amounts of information about each other, only some of which they're aware of. As soon as this human communication is reduced to the virtual world, it becomes impoverished. That's the imbalance we need to redress.

Next, we'll turn to the first of the big five problems with virtual communication.

How to read this book

The first five chapters of this book take on the five big problems with virtual communications—the lack of feedback, empathy, control, emotion, and connection—how to think about them and what to do about them. The next four chapters take on specific issues and fixes for the various digital channels: email, email alternatives, text messages, conference calls, webinars, and Skype/hangout/chat sessions. There is a final chapter on sales, since of all the important areas of human commerce, the sales side particularly depends on human connection and is perhaps most upended by the changes brought about by the virtual world. Finally, I conclude with a look at the future.

CHAPTER SUMMARY

- We humans evolved as face-to-face communicators.

- Most of our communication is unconscious and based on emotion.

- Emotion helps us determine the importance of a communication.

- Virtual communications remove most of the unconscious emotion from communication.

- With its lack of emotional content, most virtual communication is overwhelming, boring, and forgettable.

- Most forms of virtual communication don't allow the unconscious mind to do its communication work.

- We seldom make good decisions virtually.

- Research shows that when we're online, we don't work together as well as we do when we're face-to-face. We don't trust each other as much and are angrier.

- To succeed in the virtual world, we have to consciously reinsert the emotions that are missing.

PART ONE

THE FIVE BASIC PROBLEMS WITH VIRTUAL COMMUNICATIONS

THE LACK OF FEEDBACK

WHERE'S THE EMOTIONAL CLARITY?

You look at your opposite number on the negotiation team. He's sitting across the big wooden conference room table from you, and you're waiting for him to say something. Over the past four weeks, as the complicated negotiations have gone on, you've gotten to know him well. You know his tells, his nearly invisible body-language signs about what he's really thinking underneath that impassive exterior.

Finally, he says it: "I think we should go ahead." But something is nagging at you. You know his body language well enough now to pick up on subtle discomfort. You know that he's not entirely satisfied with the deal. So instead of saying, "Great, welcome aboard," you pause.

"Is there anything we haven't talked about that is making you uncomfortable?" You know there is; you want to give him a chance to voice his reservations.

And so he does. Later on, when you've ironed out the problems that were indeed still there, just beneath the surface, he confesses that he had been about to put the deal on hold and let it quietly die. He had grown to like you in the month you had been negotiating together, and he was uncomfortable with sharing what seemed like minor problems. But added together, they had become one big deal killer. If you hadn't given him the opening, he would have been ready to leave the table. Your reading of his body language saved the day.

What is that sensory feedback, and why is it so important to us humans?

There are two kinds of feedback: implicit and explicit. The implicit kind is illustrated by the example just above. It's the sensory feedback that our unconscious minds give us 24-7, the sights, sounds, smells, touches, and tastes of our world of experience. In addition to the five senses that we're all keenly aware of, neuroscientists debate a number of others, such as thermoception, proprioception, nociception, equilibrioception, mechanoreception, chemoreceptors of various kinds, hunger and thirst, and others we're just learning about.[1]

Explicit feedback is the running commentary that drives individuals, teams, and organizations to get things done from day to day. In the real world, the two kinds of feedback mix in a way that usually feels effortless. Our words are conveyed to other people—and theirs to us—with a welter of largely unconscious sensory data that automatically goes with the words. We smile, frown, draw back, lean in, laugh, and cry. Our senses are at work all the time, creating both context and emotional meaning for our daily lives.

Put us in the virtual world, and almost all these senses are deprived. Now, when the multichannel sensory system that is the brain is deprived of one or more of those senses, the neuroscientists tell us, it hates the vacuum. So, the brain fills the empty channels with assumptions, memories, and fake data. The result is, not surprisingly, all the misunderstandings we're so familiar with in the virtual world. The email that conveys a sarcastic tone the sender didn't intend. The phone conference that left everyone believing that the project was dead in the water. The video-conference that made you feel less comfortable about joining the team. Trolling. And so on.

Put us in the virtual world, in short, and we're short-changed on the implicit feedback that is so important for getting us through our days. Remember, in evolutionary terms, we humans are fragile creatures and so have developed extraordinary prediction skills and pattern-recognition abilities. We put those two skills together to keep ourselves alive. Take away the data that allows us to predict and to recognize, and we feel lost, unsafe, and confused. That's the virtual world in a nutshell.

But the issues go further. Explicit feedback relies on implicit feedback much more than most people realize. So, when we're asked what we thought of that presentation, that meeting, or that town hall session, we can offer a mix of explicit and implicit feedback. The mix allows us to soften the harsh messages and toughen the soft ones. We may only say, "It was fine," but our body language—the implicit feedback—conveys that we really thought the session was a disaster. Or the reverse. We can deliver some tough words but soften their impact with a touch or a smile that says, "It really wasn't that bad." And there are, of course, a whole host of shades of meaning possible in between.

The manager who is used to offering minimal explicit feedback because she conveys a strong connection to her team nonverbally may find herself struggling in the virtual world, where she suddenly has to articulate everything that she previously could leave unsaid. If she fails to do so, then she risks leaving her team confused about her intentions and their performance.

Take out the implicit feedback on which the explicit messages depend, and you get confusion and alienation. Let's further explore the difficulties inherent in feedback in the virtual world. We've identified the basic problem: explicit feedback relies on implicit feedback to provide the emotional connections that make human relationships matter, that help people function effectively through the daily ups and downs of organizational life, and that help them endure.

Explicit feedback lacks the unconscious context of human emotional exchange

All too often online, feedback becomes trolling and rapidly descends into hate on all sides. Why is that? Why does this honorable form of human commentary from one person to another rarely work online?

Fundamentally, what has changed is the nature of trust. And as trust changes, so do the relationships, precisely because of how we are hardwired to form connections with people. Trust in the virtual world is much more fragile, though perhaps easier to establish initially. But the big difference comes when something threatens the trust.

And feedback depends on trust. In face-to-face relationships where there is trust, one party may do something to screw up, causing friction, anger, and even a bit of mistrust to creep in. But if the connection is strong enough, the feedback begins. The issue will get thrashed out, the perpetrator will apologize, and trust will be restored. Indeed, once restored, the trust may be stronger than ever.

How different it is in the virtual world! Once trust is threatened, it's instantly broken, and it's nearly impossible to reestablish it. People simply move on. Since trust was more fragile in the first place, it shatters with very little provocation.

Thus, virtual feedback has some obvious flaws. First of all, there's much less of it because virtual feedback is simply harder to give than is face-to-face feedback. Second, virtual feedback is less robust and more likely to cause irreparable harm. And third, the resultant weaker feedback has much less meaning.

There's less spontaneous virtual feedback because trust is more fragile. Why should I enter into the first half of a feedback loop if my trust in you is not very deep and liable to be eventually broken inadvertently even if it isn't broken deliberately?

Lacking the unconscious stream of emotional information we receive automatically from other people face-to-face, online communication and feedback is much less robust, much less compelling, and indeed much less interesting than face-to-face feedback. But it still can sting.

Why does online feedback hurt so much? We humans are social beings; put us face-to-face, and we share mirror neurons that allow us to match each other's emotions unconsciously and immediately.[2] We leak emotions to each other. We anticipate and mirror each other's movements when we're in sympathy or agreement with one another—when we're on the same side. And we can mirror each other's brain activity when we're engaged in storytelling and listening—both halves of the communication conundrum.[3]

All of that leaking and sharing creates trust, intimacy, and connection. It creates receptivity and interest in the other person's point of view.

We want to achieve this state of human communion; it's a mistake to think that most humans prefer the solitary life that so much of modern virtual life imposes on us. We are most comfortable when we're connected, sharing strong emotions and stories, and led by a strong, charismatic leader who is keeping us safe and together.

The virtual world, in contrast, is much less engaging. We humans are much less engaged in most forms of this world because the forms lack the emotional information we crave.

Negative virtual feedback hurts

Beyond trust or the lack of it, another demand has arisen concomitantly in the virtual face-to-face mix we live in today: authenticity. We live in an era when the demand for authenticity trumps a number of qualities that society used to deem more important. Authenticity has always had a measure of importance, but its stock has risen and fallen depending on the times. Right now, it beats out excellence, coolness, and artifice; to jump to the top of the charts or the best-seller list, you have to be ready to open up.

The demand for authenticity makes you more vulnerable to (and more exposed to) feedback. And online feedback is far more often of the trolling kind. The result is the naming and shaming, the Twitter wars, the instant celebrities whose lives are just as instantly ruined by hate-filled outpourings of online denizens who pounce virtually on those who put themselves out there.

And thus we become febrile inhabitants of a world that is deeply reflective of the ironies of our times: we crave feedback, and yet we fear it. It is both wonderful and soul-killing. We are insecure and immune. We have celebrities and politicians who are more loved and more hated than ever before.

We crave recognition and fear it at the same time. We are polarized. We are tribal. We are addicted to the feedback—the recognition, the likes, the retweets, the confirmation of the virtual world—and are terrified that it will turn on us and destroy us.

Trust in the virtual world is not only fragile, but also a weapon. And yet we need to trust, because we are one click away from identity theft, or trolling, or worse: oblivion.

Just try to deprive someone of their mobile phone. The very thought has given rise to a new social disease. As many as 66 percent of adults may suffer from it.[4] For some, the anxiety is so severe that it can cause panic attacks. But almost everyone in modern society has this problem to some degree. What's going on?

It's called nomophobia—no-mobile-phone-phobia.[5] Researchers have recently coined the term to describe the fear of being without your smartphone. If you've ever had a moment of panic when you checked your pocket or purse and your phone wasn't where you thought it was, if the sight of a low-battery warning freaks you out, if you can't imagine leaving the house without your phone, if you never turn it off, if you no longer know how to survive three minutes in a grocery store checkout line without checking your phone, you may have nomophobia.

Caglar Yildirim and Ana-Paula Correia, researchers from Iowa State University, have identified four main components of nomophobia: "not being able to communicate, losing connectedness, not being able to access information, and giving up convenience."[6] The inability to communicate with friends and loved ones is the most obvious and understandable reason to worry about being without a smartphone. But the phobia goes beyond just concern about staying connected. The questionnaire the researchers used to "diagnose" nomophobia also asked people to respond to statements like "Being unable to get the news on my smartphone would make me nervous" and "I would be nervous because I would be disconnected from my online identity."

Think about that. Our social media personas have become so central to our lives that the idea of being disconnected from them makes us nervous. Psychologists say that loneliness and insecurity contribute to this problem.[7] It makes sense—in the age of the smartphone, you never have to be truly alone. You can always text or tweet or post on Facebook and instantly feel the warmth of human connection.

Or the terror of trolling. That's the Catch-22 of the virtual world and the need for, and dread of, feedback.

But there's even more going on here. Relying on our smartphones is actually reshaping our brains. Research shows that when we can easily get information from an external source, we gradually lose our ability to remember that information. Think about it. How many phone numbers do you know by heart? If you wanted to know the name of the actor who played that guy in that movie about the train, would you rack your brain, ask a friend, debate it for twenty minutes—or just google it?

If your phone has become part of your brain, it's no wonder you feel anxious to be without it. And this problem is only going to grow. Younger people are already more likely to suffer from nomophobia than are older generations. More than three-quarters of people aged eighteen to twenty-four have nomophobia, compared with 66 percent for older folks.[8] One survey found that 92 percent of teenagers never turn off their phones.[9] And when teens were separated from their phones, their blood pressure rose, and they didn't perform as well on simple cognitive tests of things like memory and attention as they did when they had their phones.

These young people need to have their phones with them just to feel normal. Is this the digital mastery we thought we were going to achieve in the digital era?

Without emotional subtext, we become less competent

Digital confusion, not digital competence, reigns supreme today. How many times have you unintentionally started a virtual war with a colleague or friend over a minor misunderstanding of tone and have it quickly escalate into a full-blown snit? You were moving fast, you forgot to mention that your colleague actually had a week to complete the project, and—while you did your best to repair the damage—you looked thoughtless at best.

At the heart of this sort of miscommunication and many others like it is a lack of quick, effortless, face-to-face feedback. In person, the twitch of an eyebrow or a quizzical smile is all it takes to signal that your attempt at humor fell flat. But in the virtual world, timely feedback is usually missing. By the time you get feedback, it's because the other party is furious, hurt, or ready to cancel the sale.

Further, the pressure to move quickly can often mean we lose track of important details in the rush to answer an email or move a project along. Details get lost, implications that normally could be conveyed with a tone of voice go unheard, and resentments flair.

Let's go back to first principles. A successful communication is not a monologue; it's a conversation. And a conversation is always two-way. There's always a feedback loop, at minimum. To put it another way, if participants don't have the sense that others are listening to them, then they won't feel part of the communication and it won't succeed.

The realities of twenty-first-century work life, especially post-2008, means that many of us have more virtual meetings throughout our work lives than we have face-to-face ones. This difference represents a huge shift in organizational life—and human behavior—in less than a generation. Of course, the purveyors of the high-tech equipment that makes these meetings possible tout the benefits—efficiency, speed, savings on travel, and so on. These are undeniable.

But virtual meetings will never replace the need for humans to exchange emotional and unconscious nonverbal information through face-to-face exchanges. Virtual communication can make do, but that's all, and it won't work for difficult conversations, important transactions, highly emotional discussions, and most other kinds of important feedback—any time strong human emotions are involved.

Virtual meetings are second-best: trust is hard, and feedback is either lacking or hurtful

Think about why an online organization like Amazon has such high trust ratings, whereas many others do not. Amazon puts a ferocious amount of effort into ensuring that you always have a good, transparent transaction when you go on the site. And shopping is just about the easiest form of human interaction.

But for everything else, I wonder if we are changing something basic about how we form relationships. Will the next generations be able to invest in online connections the same way that everyone now invests in "real" face-to-face relationships?

If most of your relationships are virtual, their fragility may make you less able to get through the bumps and shocks that every (face-to-face) relationship naturally endures. If you take the pattern of commitment from the virtual world, your understanding of the meaning of relationship will be attenuated and weak. What will trust and feedback look like then?

Today, you need to sharpen your communication skills. You need to become a much more effective communicator by entering each conversation, virtual or digital, with a clear picture of your goals for the interaction and what you need from the other person. You also have to know how to get reliable, regular feedback by verbally asking someone to check your progress whenever you cannot obtain unconscious feedback from face-to-face contact.

Here are a few basic rules for mastering the digital version of feedback—information that, in the face-to-face world, is such a simple mix of explicit and implicit reactions.

Virtual feedback should be appropriate to the effort, to the occasion, and to the recipient. Tact is important, but so is honesty. Every year when the TV program *American Idol* aired, the show began with hilarious outtakes of truly terrible singers stomping off in fury after one or another of the judges told them, gently or bluntly, that they were indeed terrible. Often, it was clear from the comments of all concerned that no one had ever given these painfully bad singers any honest feedback before. As a result, they had been permitted to nurse hopeless dreams of stardom, often for years, until the contestants were brought up short by reality in the form of national television humiliation. They were furious, hurt, and sometimes in denial, but there was no question about the appropriateness of the feedback. They had set themselves up for it; judgment was what they were there for. Indeed, that was the inescapable point of the show.

Virtual feedback should be honest, but it doesn't need to be cruel. Teachers and other early influencers often bear the responsibility of giving feedback to no-hopers, or people aspiring to something that the teachers feel is unattainable. And for the most part, the influencers are doing the underachievers and the rest of the world a favor directing them into other lines of work. But occasionally, one of those no-hopers turns out to be a Twyla Tharp or a Picasso or a Steve Jobs. For all those future geniuses, as well as the rest of us, it's important to leaven clarity with kindness.

Virtual feedback should be both authoritative and humble. Again, for the future geniuses who have repeatedly proven the early critics wrong, those giving feedback should be aware of their own shortcomings as artists, business geniuses, or chess players themselves. If you do offer feedback, have some basis for your judgment, some real claim to expertise. And you should also understand the limits of that expertise and weigh your words accordingly.

Virtual feedback should be specific and focused on the relevant object, performance, or creation. If you perceive work to be slapdash, say so, and explain how it falls short, but don't conclude that the creator is lazy. A failed artistic performance doesn't entitle you to judge the character of the performer. And general comments are far less useful—and far more damaging—than specific ones. Don't say, "This seems off to me." Rather, do the hard work of perceiving and then saying, "The brush strokes in the upper part of the painting seem to me to be conveying a sense of urgency that's lacking in the lower part." Or something like that.

Virtual feedback should never be more about the giver than the recipient. Go to a writer's meet-up group, and you'll hear mystery writers telling nonfiction writers that their work needs more suspense. Inevitably, feedback takes the form all too often of talking to oneself—the feedback really concerns what the giver knows at some deep level to be the problem with his or her own work. If you're going to offer feedback, you have to have enough security, distance, and impartiality to deliver an opinion that is truly helpful. If the receiver feels seen, then this recognition goes a long way to mitigating the painful feelings surrounding the criticism.

Virtual feedback is an obligation that the previous generation or class owes the next one. If humans don't improve, they merely reinvent the art or business wheel, and when they do that, they doom themselves or their organizations to the rubbish heap of history. Both the business world and the art world are ruthlessly competitive. We all need to bring our best games to the match.

Feedback should be offered in generosity and received in humility. Both giving and receiving feedback involve vulnerability and risk. The participants need to respect and honor each other. If the participants lack these qualities of generosity and humility, then the feedback process is generally either useless or destructive.

Those seven guidelines summarize what feedback should be. As you have no doubt experienced, the reality often falls short in the face-to-face world. In the virtual world, lacking the support of implicit feedback, explicit feedback is often devastating for the recipient.

Practical fixes

The virtual triage list

A triage list for communications feedback will help prevent the all-too-frequent misunderstandings in the virtual world. Use this list to create the feedback habit for audioconferences, video connections, and so on.

1. What is the point of this communication or exchange?

2. What do I want to get out of the exchange?

3. What does the other person or group want out of the exchange?

4. How did I feel at the beginning of the exchange?

5. How did I feel at the end?

6. How did the other party or parties feel at the beginning of the exchange?

7. Did I enquire?

8. How did the other party or parties feel at the end of the exchange?

9. Did I enquire?

10. Did I summarize the gist of the exchange?

11. Did I check for misunderstandings?

12. What, if anything, should I do differently the next time?

The emoji summary

Begin a virtual communication (e.g., an audioconference or a videoconference) by sending out one of several emoji, or symbols, agreed on in advance by your team, to indicate your emotional state at the start of the communication. Have the entire team check in this way. (There's a reason why emoji and emoticons have flourished in the virtual world—precisely because they add back the missing emotional elements. You need to learn to make this practice deliberate and habitual.) Green, yellow, and red, for example, could mean, respectively, "all good," "it's not a great day; I'm a little stressed," and "all hell is breaking loose," or "something serious is wrong on my end."

Then finish your virtual meeting by reporting green, yellow, and red again. If necessary, follow up for clarification.

The feedback cheat sheet

Review the following list often, ideally before you give feedback each time, to make sure you are offering your opinion effectively.

1. Feedback should be appropriate to the effort, to the occasion, and to the recipient.

2. Feedback should be honest, but it doesn't need to be cruel.

3. It should be both authoritative and humble.

4. It should be specific and focused on the relevant object, performance, or creation.

5. Feedback should never be more about the giver than the recipient.

6. Feedback is an obligation that the previous generation or class owes the next one.

7. Feedback should be offered in generosity and received in humility.

8. Feedback, like trust, falls apart in virtual exchanges because it lacks the unconscious context of human emotional exchange; so consciously restore the emotions in an exchange.

CHAPTER SUMMARY

- Feedback—both implicit and explicit—is an essential part of the face-to-face world.

- In the virtual world, feedback becomes much more fraught with misunderstanding.

- Trust is more fragile online and is essential for feedback; otherwise, the feedback becomes trolling.

- We crave the human connection in both the real and the virtual worlds, but the virtual connection is less satisfying, so our cravings are never satisfied—and negative feedback is more surprising and hurtful.

- As a result, we both overindulge in virtual forms of communication and feel more lonely.

- We should increase the emotional clarity of our online communications by giving agreed-upon signals communicating our emotional intents and attitudes, at both the beginning and the end of virtual communications.

THE LACK OF EMPATHY

WHERE'S THE CONSISTENCY?

Recently, I was introduced to a potential business connection by a mutual friend, and we decided to connect on Skype for an initial chat. I had entered the information incorrectly into my calendar, so it was a bit late by the time I got everything straightened out and we connected. I was frazzled by the experience, and on top of my distractions, the Skype connection was unusually poor; it kept winking in and out.

I could see—and sense viscerally—that my potential connection might be giving up. Here was this late, frazzled, technologically incompetent person. Why bother? I wanted to say, "The impression you're getting—that's not me! I'm usually cool, I'm technologically competent, and I'm nearly always on time. A completely different person!"

The connection did not thrive, and no business resulted. In person, I could have rushed in, obviously sweating and harried, and explained it away with an excuse that would at least have been human. And we might have survived the experience. My personal presence might have compensated for my tardiness.

Online relationships must go well, or they won't go at all

Online, there is no chance. As the old saw has it, if I do something stupid, it's because I'm having a bad day. If you do something stupid, it's because of a character flaw. That's desperately true online.

Openness is incredibly important in getting relationships off to a good start. And openness that works with humans is all about sending welcoming signals with your face, torso, hands, and body, without overdoing it or crowding the personal space of the other person too much. How do you do that online?

You can't. An unintended consequence of our new, amazing, superconvenient virtual world, where everything (almost everything) is a few clicks away, is that it robs us of real closeness. More than that, by spending time online, we lose out on intimacy. Facebook, your favorite airline rewards program, and even Amazon take away that real closeness as fast as they offer us faux intimacy. This world knows who our friends are! It knows the kind of seat and meal we want! It can recommend books to us that we might want to buy!

But even the thrilling sight of a new box from Amazon will never replace the crinkling around a true friend's eyes when you tell him or her about your adventures on your last vacation—or your last trip into town. The friend who knows all the disasters that befell you on the trip before that.

All those delightful likes, wows, and loves on Facebook in the end simply make us hungry for more. The virtual world is a never-ending banquet that never completely satisfies. The loop is never closed. The internet doesn't hug you back. The virtual world fails to deliver on a basic human need: empathy. This emotional connection between us helps glue the whole human experiment together.

Consistency in communications is even more important in the virtual world than it is in the face-to-face world

In the real world, when a team decides to take a difficult action—to commit to extra hours to get a project done, for example—the team leader can judge the level of resistance by noting the body language around the table. The leader might offer time off, say, after the project is done, to mollify the unhappy faces around the room.

But something odd happens to informed consent in the virtual world. Here, without the visual element of those unhappy faces, the team leader *hears* only silence, and silence implies consent. So, the likelihood that the real feelings of the team won't get expressed rises exponentially.

It's another form of empathy failure. The distance provided by a virtual connection creates conditions where people are much more likely to behave badly to one another and are much less likely to be sympathetic to others' feelings. There's a lack of empathy.

Sandy Pentland at MIT has found that communications on teams works best when all participants communicate in roughly equal measure.[1] That's very hard to get right in the virtual world—on those endless conference calls, for example.

You know the ones, where you've got your mute button on so that you can practice the tuba while the boss is nattering on about something—again. Nothing seems to happen for huge stretches of time, so out comes the tuba.

On the rare occasions when you actually either want to or have to participate, you wake up, put down the tuba, and lunge for the mute button, so that you can add your two virtual cents. But the boss has already moved on.

You wanted to say something, but the ship of protest has sailed and it's too late. Assumed consent will take over, and your options are narrowing fast. The digital world robs us of our human reactions and thus a little bit of our humanity in moments like this—something we never get back.

Email diminishes us as well. In an email message, we can't show all the nuances we would with a raised eyebrow, a slight smile, or a shake of the head in person. We settle for just a little bit less.

Our humanity is diminished in the virtual world

Add in video, and it doesn't get any better. On videoconferences, the artificiality of the exchange is brought home to us. We tend to shout, to cut other people off, and to tire quickly on video. Our unconscious minds are not receiving the information we would get in person about how close or far away the other person is. Thus, we overcompensate. It's like trying to have an intimate conversation with someone who is standing on the other side of one of those old-fashioned glass ticket windows. You can't quite see clearly. You can't quite hear. And you can't quite measure with your other senses what's going on. It's exhausting. And so a little bit of you resigns itself to being a little less present. Once again, empathy is diminished.

There is no virtual communication vehicle or channel that works as well as the in-person variety. Less of us gets through to the other person. We are a little blind, a little deaf, and a little less human in every virtual setting. Digital communication channels were designed by engineers, remember. Not orators or extroverts or even politicians.

OK, that was a cheap shot. But how can we regain our diminished humanity in the digital space?

The key to understanding this conundrum is empathy, the human emotion that connects us to each other. When we are face-to-face, even the coldest of us find our mirror neurons firing when we are with someone who is experiencing an emotion. We laugh together, cry together, bond together. Put us in the virtual space, and empathy can't work as well. The mirror neurons don't fire as readily. We remain disassociated.

We humans need our empathy

A recent study found that regular face-to-face communication cuts the risk of depression in adults by half. Phone and email don't have the same effect.[2]

Our unconscious minds need to get together so that they can find the emotional connections they crave. We humans are social beings. We don't do well when deprived of our fellow humans.

We need to feed the unconscious, and we starve it at our peril as employers, as employees, and as humans. The virtual world is boring for our unconscious minds. We need face-to-face.

I work with people to help them decide on the persona they want to put across in their conversations, meetings, and presentations, and even these people and I struggle to talk about what we mean by the concept of a persona. When I ask people how they would like to be perceived, they use terms like *authoritative, funny, expert, approachable, confident,* and *humble.* The list goes on, but I'm always struck by how impoverished our language is to talk about this very important business of how others take us.

Mostly, people list positive adjectives—who would list negative ones?—and then we discuss what their behavior is likely to inspire now, what the gap is, and how to get to the desired state. How to be more empathetic, or confident, or authoritative, or funny, or expert for an audience.

How do you project emotions?

Letting your emotions show is slow, painstaking work. Take empathy. How do you appear to be more empathetic? What does that mean, exactly? And can you do it at all online?

Presumably, the word *empathy* suggests sensitivity to the feelings of others. How do you project that quality from a stage? Or across a room? Is it a tilt of the head, a hand gesture, a posture, or something you say? And is everyone struck the same way by your attempts at appearing more empathetic?

In person, we can be empathetic automatically, because of our mirror neuron system. Online, the mirror neuron system can't work as well. So, what happens?

A recent study found that you can increase people's empathy—specifically for others' suffering—by having them touch rough sandpaper.[3] That little bit of discomfort makes us more aware of discomfort in general and thus more sensitive to others' potential discomfort.

It's a fascinating study, but it shows us how little we understand about a feeling like empathy and what drives it. If a momentary encounter with sandpaper can make people measurably more empathetic, how is that feeling generated to begin with? And more importantly, how driven is it by our physicality rather than what we normally think of as our psychology?

Now apply that insight to the virtual world. If most of our humanity is driven, as it seems to be, by literal metaphors from the real world, how can we expect to thrive in the virtual? It's not just sandpaper. If you give us a hot cup of coffee to hold, we form warmer opinions of brief images of people we see online. Holding something cold has the opposite effect.[4] There are many such examples. Our brains are hardwired for real sensory data, not ersatz. And given that we can increase people's empathy with applications to the physical senses, what implications does that have for manipulating people's perceptions of empathy online?

A few principles are in order here. Our physical and mental experiences are deeply interconnected. We're only beginning to understand this relationship. Our nascent understanding alone should make us wary of the virtual world.

Our attitudes, emotions, and intentions are mostly *unconscious*. When you make me rub my finger on rough sandpaper, I become more empathetic, but not because I've consciously thought something like, "Oh, that sandpaper is rough; therefore, I should be more sympathetic to others' pain." It's rather an unconscious and emotional connection. And it's more powerful precisely because we're not conscious of it.

The physical experience opens us up to the mental, rather than the other way around. At one level, that's obvious; we are physical beings, after all. But at a deeper level, the connection between the physical and the emotional tells us something profound about how the mind works, something counterintuitive and puzzling.

We embody our emotions. We move with attraction, with revulsion, with happiness, with sorrow. And only once we begin to move do we become aware of and understand what we're thinking.

Finally, our attitudes, emotions, and intentions are profoundly communal and tribal. We experience empathy, and all those other adjectives I listed earlier, as our attitudes toward others and as others' attitudes toward us. We like to think of ourselves as self-directed, individual, and conscious. What we're learning is that humans are instead connected, unconscious, and tribal beings. That's our empathy. And that's what is missing in the virtual world.

The entire virtual world was supposed to increase our interconnectedness, but instead it has isolated us more because our emotional engines don't work as well on the information super-highway. In teenagers, there is a direct correlation between mobile phone use and depression. The more time they spend on the phone, the more depressed they are.[5] We need to learn new communications approaches to the digital real world we live in today.

What is the life cycle of empathy online?

The problem of empathy plays out through the entire business relationship. Imagine the kind of business relationship where one party is the service or product provider and the other party is the client or customer. There's choice involved; the customer could walk away as desired and choose another vendor. In some sort of initial set of meetings, ideas are pitched, prices are nego-tiated, and other issues are hammered out. A deal is struck, and the work proceeds.

The engagement might last a year, more or less. There are ups and downs along the way; communication by its nature involves miscommunication. Problems somehow get straightened out. Baggage is accumulated, but on the whole, the work gets done, the bills get paid, and the client is reasonably happy.

If it's a large contract with lots of players, then there will be individual stories along with the main story about the two teams interacting. People will cycle on and off, leave their jobs, leave town, have children, move to Seattle to take care of an aged par-ent, and so on.

But what is the life cycle of the main relationship? There will be three main stages, followed by a fourth, the winding-down stage. The stages can overlap and perhaps even restart in various ways, but overall, they go forward with the arrow of time. And each will have its corresponding form of empathy.

Stage 1: Decide on friend or foe. The first stage is the relationship-establishing or deal-killing friend-or-foe analysis. Neuroscience tells us that the first thing people do when they get together is decide on a few questions: Do I feel comfortable with this person? Is this person a friend or a foe? Some people rub us the wrong way from the start. Others we click with immediately. Those determinations are largely made by our unconscious minds—and they're made quickly. That's the way it works face-to-face.

We can override our unconscious, so-called gut feelings, or not. We can have our individual reaction swallowed up in the team reaction as a whole. Or we can carry the day. There are all sorts of possible outcomes, but basically our unconscious minds are going to decide on friend or foe, and we can't stop ourselves from making that fundamental calibration.

It will affect everything that follows. If we decide on friend, then the relationship is off to a good start and the several stages that follow will have a better chance of working well, too. If we decide the person is a foe, then everything that follows will become much more difficult. Communication miscues will be far more common, and our enthusiasm for the subsequent stages will diminish, perhaps precipitously.

The online version of this establishing step is much more difficult to get right. Because the emotional exchanges are muted or shut out completely, the relationship, even at its best, is tepid. You cannot easily establish a strong sense of empathy. And trust is thus fragile. Or the brain will simply make up the emotions it imagines the other person is experiencing, because the unconscious brain hates an information vacuum.

Here's the main lesson: If you can possibly begin a relationship of any importance in person, you should do so. Period, full stop, end of discussion.

If, for a variety of reasons, you can't, then be aware that the relationship will be far more fragile than it otherwise might have been. Do everything you can, especially early on, to be consistent, trustworthy, and transparent. Any cracks in that edifice will doom the relationship.

Stage 2: Establish credibility. The next stage is the credibility stage. That's where we decide, if we're the client, Does this vendor know what it (or he or she) is talking about? This stage can take a little longer or a lot longer than the first stage, depending on the cultures involved (how fast people get down to business) and the deliberate opportunities scheduled early on for establishing credibility, say, with a workshop or training session. If we are a vendor, we make a similar decision, but it might be more accurately phrased as, Does this person or team have the right power, access, and competencies?

This credibility check is the only stage of a virtual business relationship that can thrive at least as well as a face-to-face one can. The information explosion that is the internet allows us to check, double-check, and triple-check a party's expertise, bona fides, and arrest record.

Stage 3: Establish trust. Once the first two phases are accomplished, the work can begin. We have entered the trust phase. It's the longest of the three phases, simply because this stage is when the work is being done, but also because trust takes time to establish. We want to see how a person or group reacts under different conditions, including stress. We may even test the party for reliability. Does the person or group come through for us under unusual circumstances? Do they work late to make us look good? Do they cut ethical corners under certain conditions? And on and on.

If the trust is violated or broken at some point, people naturally fall back on competence. We will continue the relationship if the estimation of competence is high enough to overcome the broken trust. If not, the relationship can irrevocably break down.

Online, this stage remains fragile, without the durability of a face-to-face friendship. For this reason, it's more difficult to create the trust and easier to break it. Once again, an empathy deficit is the cause.

Stage 4: The relationship winds down. The final stage is a natural winding down of the relationship. The ending may be strictly defined by a work calendar or, less precisely, by a sense that the goals set at the beginning have been accomplished. If the work has been successful and the personal connections strong, there may even be continued connection long after the basic work is done. Online, the ending is more abrupt and people rarely return to talk over the experience.

The online world needs to sip from the emotional well

The very nature of the virtual world further chips away at the traditional human connections of a business relationship. One negative influence of the online world is simply, for example, the distractions of daily virtual life. A second one is how some online memes go viral.

As has been observed countless times by countless people, we live in an increasingly overstimulated, 24-7, interruption-prone world. We check email hundreds of times a day and Facebook more often than that.

Thus, we are constantly pulled away from the present moment and are pushed into our heads, our mobile phones, and our to-do lists. When we have the opportunity to meet someone new, the impression that we're likely to give ranges from not fully present to actively distracted. It's not a good continuum to be on. The other party will unconsciously sense the distraction—or perhaps even consciously—and feel resentment as a result. Relationships can get off to a weak or fragile start in that way, particularly online.

In face-to-face encounters, though, there's a chance that our unconscious minds will take over and make the relationship real even though our conscious minds aren't paying much attention. But online, there is no fallback. We tend to start out badly in the virtual world, and doubly so, because we're usually blissfully unaware of how poorly it's going. Because empathy is unconscious, we don't notice its absence as quickly as we would if it were a conscious experience. What can we do to put the essentially human back into the virtual?

Think about what goes viral online: the simple, the emotional, the repetitive, the cotton candy of the mind. If we spend our days dipping in and out of that trivial stream of data, we are impoverished in any deeper emotional sense. And over time, this propensity will cheapen our online lives—and our experience of empathy.

But we can do better. If we dig deep into stories that offer the raw power of human emotion and struggle and if we guide online audiences on a journey into real intimacy and connection, then we will truly engage them. We will provide an experience that begins to restore some of the emotions that the virtual takes out, and we'll create a strong bond of empathy.

What sort of a journey will you take your virtual audience on? Will you tell them a love story? Will it be a quest for understanding or growth or mastery? Will it be a journey of discovery in a strange new land? Will it be a tale of hard-won success after much struggle? You have the power of choice, but you can't duck the responsibility of digging deeper than anyone else does today to find the unique, human story that only you can tell—and that will resonate with almost everyone you touch.[6]

We care enormously about other people's intent. What do they mean, and what do they mean toward us? Are they friend or foe? Powerful or subservient? A potential mate or not? And the questions go on.

We're more alike than we are different. Recent work on brain scans, for example, can read human emotions with 90 percent accuracy. Researchers showed people pictures of unpleasant things—physical injuries, hate groups, and acts of aggression—and found that people reacted in predictable ways. But more than that, they all reacted with pretty much the same brain patterns.[7]

We're more alike than we are different

Similarly, work by a team of psychologists at Princeton University found that when a storyteller and a listener get together, their brain patterns match up identically. Stories take over our brains—and in the same ways.[8]

Human emotions are similar, and the brain patterns show it. As the Princeton study's chief researcher, Luke Chang, put it, emotions have a "neural signature," which is essentially the same from human to human. The study's findings also suggest that computers could learn to recognize these emotions with high accuracy—90 percent so far. The *2001: A Space Odyssey* scenario is not as far off as we might like to think.

The price of online attention is distraction

But just getting a hearing in the minds of harried, overstimulated consumers is increasingly difficult. Your new product, new service, or new marketplace approach—all of it has to compete with a thousand other such stories and a thousand other sources of information, entertainment, and distraction.

Your story will have to be more compelling than the alternatives. That's not easy, especially given the inherent limits on storytelling online in service to a commercial idea. Commercially aimed stories are not pure storytelling; they don't want to risk controversy, and among other features, they are biased toward the happy ending.

A whole industry is developing around software that is learning to recognize human emotion—more precisely and accurately than humans can. With such technology becoming available, your corporate story will have to stand up to competing stories that will be tested against the split-second emotional reactions of potential customers. Soon, software will understand the emotional reactions and decisions of your customers better than any human can.

A by-product of this research is that we're learning how much of decision making is unconscious and is indeed beyond the reach of the conscious mind until the decision is already made.[9] Your traditional means of testing—the focus groups, the in-depth interviews, the surveys, and so on—by their very nature miss out on the interesting parts of consumer choice. If you're not tapping into this new kind of data, you're not only behind the curve, but also out of the loop, the one that matters, the consumer decision-making loop.

Can your story stand up to that kind of pressure? Does your story meet these new kinds of tests?

Moreover, you now have to tell your story faster and faster. Impossible to tell a great story in a few seconds, you say? Apparently, Ernest Hemingway (to win a luncheon bet, the tale goes) told perhaps the shortest story ever and inadvertently started a flash-fiction game that has gone on to this day: six-word stories. His (the story goes) example: *For sale: baby shoes, never worn.*

The story may be apocryphal, but the point stands. Short stories can have punch.

In the virtual world, good storytelling is even more important

Some new research into the unconscious workings of the mind points toward cracking this code of storytelling in the digital world in a way that will grab people and not let them go.[10] How do you do that? Ezequiel Morsella, the theory's lead author, puts it this way: "The information we perceive in our consciousness is not created by conscious processes, nor is it reacted to by conscious processes. Consciousness is the middle-man, and it doesn't do as much work as you think."[11]

We may feel like we're in charge of our minds, effortlessly having those conscious feelings, thoughts, and ideas that seem to lead naturally to our actions. But as Morsella says, "we have long thought consciousness solved problems and had many moving parts, but it's much more basic and static. This theory is very counterintuitive. It goes against our everyday way of thinking."

Instead, our conscious minds are simply acting, watching, and reporting to ourselves on our repetitive movements over and over again—walking, eating, chasing after saber-toothed cats—just another day at the caveperson office. The important decisions driving those actions are taken by the unconscious mind and sent up to the conscious mind to become aware of and move on. As Morsella puts it, "for the vast majority of human history, we were hunting and gathering and had more pressing concerns that required rapidly executed voluntary actions. Consciousness seems to have evolved for these types of actions rather than to understand itself."[12]

This evolutionary result makes sense, because unconscious thought is more efficient than conscious thought. So as a species, we're always trying to articulate our feelings and telling people to get in touch with them, but those feelings are doing quite well unconsciously. Unconscious thought is simply faster and may have saved your life on more than one occasion. It's just that it isn't conscious.

Online, your hands are tied behind your back

But the unconscious doesn't work very well online. Unconscious thought and gestures *precede* conscious thought. In fact, so important is gesture—a physical manifestation of our unconscious—that we find it hard to communicate if we are unable to gesture. Try speaking for any length of time with your hands tied behind your back, either literally or figuratively. You'll find it surprisingly difficult.

Think of the online consequences. Your hands are *always* virtually tied behind your back.

Face-to-face, we're always signaling, and so is everyone else, about intentions and feelings. Most of the time, we pay no conscious attention to all those signals—either the ones we're putting out or the ones others are sending to us. Our unconscious handles all that. Online, the signaling is restricted, muted, and at times completely absent. We're not consciously aware of the absence, but unconsciously, the paucity of the communications channel, whether it's text based, voice based, or even visual, frustrates us and makes us feel incomplete.

What can you do to improve the paucity of online human connection and thus the essential exchange of empathy that drives so much else in human behavior? First of all, increase your own efforts to be emotionally transparent and authentic. Precisely because the online world is emotionally less satisfying—the emotional equivalent of Pringles, so you have to keep dipping back into the can to get more, because a few don't satisfy—you have to become clearer in your own mind on what you intend, what you expect, and what you require.

Second, increase your efforts to demand the same emotional clarity of others. Once you've stepped up your efforts, you then can expect others to do the same. Remember, to a much greater extent, you are what you say you are online. In person, we can check what people say against their body language for consistency, but online, we tend to take people and institutions at their word—provisionally. Of course, at the first sign of inconsistency, we sever the connection. Which makes the third step critical.

Third, regularly test your online expressions and connections by asking: Are they authentic, clear, complete, and consistent? Your online presence needs regular housekeeping and updating in a way that isn't so urgent in person. In person, you can say to a business connection, "We're updating our brochure." But in the virtual world, your website, your Facebook presence, or any other social media identity represents who you are. Inconsistencies are damning.

I'll close with a couple of techniques for providing relief in the online emotional desert.

Practical fixes

The empathy quiz

(This test is based on one developed by Simon Baron-Cohen at the University of Cambridge.)

Give yourself a plus if you agree with each of the twenty-five statements, a minus if you don't agree. Scoring below.

1. I can easily tell if someone else wants to enter a conversation.   + —

2. I really enjoy caring for other people.   + —

3. I try to solve my own problems rather than discussing them with others.   + —

4. I find it hard to know what to do in a social situation.   + —

5. Friendships and relationships are just too difficult, so I tend not to bother with them.   + —

6. In a conversation, I tend to focus on my own thoughts rather than on what my listener might be thinking.   + —

7. I can pick up quickly if someone says one thing but means another.   + —

8. I tend to have very strong opinions about morality.   + —

9. It is hard for me to see why some things upset people so much.   + —

10. I find it easy to put myself in somebody else's shoes.   + —

11. I think that good manners are the most important thing a parent can teach a child.   + —

12. I am good at predicting how someone will feel.   + —

13. I am quick to spot when someone in a group is feeling awkward or uncomfortable.   + —

14. I am very blunt, which some people take to be rudeness, even though I don't mean to be rude.   + —

15. People tell me I am good at understanding how they are feeling and what they are thinking.   + —

16. When I talk to people, I tend to talk about their experiences rather than my own.   + —

17. I can make decisions without being influenced by others' feelings.   + —

18. I can easily tell if someone is interested or bored with what I am saying.   + —

19. Friends usually talk to me about their problems, because they say that I am very understanding.   + —

20. I can sense if I am intruding, even if the other person doesn't tell me. $+$ $-$

21. I like to be very organized in day-to-day life and often make lists of the chores I have to do. $+$ $-$

22. I can rapidly and intuitively tune into how someone else feels. $+$ $-$

23. I can easily work out what another person might want to talk about. $+$ $-$

24. I can tell if someone is masking his or her true emotion. $+$ $-$

25. I can usually appreciate the other person's viewpoint, even if I disagree with it. $+$ $-$

Score two points for a plus next to questions 1, 2, 7, 10, 12, 13, 15, 16, 18, 19, 20, 22, 23, 24, and 25. Score one point for a minus next to questions 3, 4, 5, 6, 8, 9, 11, 14, 17, and 21.

Scores:

30–40: You are highly empathetic. You will be able to fine-tune your empathy for the virtual world with ease.

20–29: You are moderately empathetic. You will sometimes find showing empathy in the virtual world difficult.

10–19: You have weak empathy. You will regularly make empathy misjudgments in the virtual world.

0–10: You have an empathy deficit. The virtual world will be an empathy minefield for you.

The virtual safe space

Every important digital connection—meetings, negotiations, and the like—needs to conclude with a time-limited, curated, virtual safe space, where participants both get and use the time to state their emotional reaction to the outcomes of the discussion. As the leader, you begin the exchange by stating a real emotional truth you're feeling in the moment, and you give everyone else the chance to do the same.

Assign an MC or chair for regular meetings

For your regular virtual staff meetings or ongoing virtual meetings that take place online, assign one person the role of MC, or chair. His or her job is to monitor the meeting in three ways. First, the MC begins by asking about everyone's emotional state—"How is everyone today?"—and then getting specific answers from all the participants. Next, the MC monitors the meeting in terms of participation. The research shows that equal participation increases satisfaction with the outcome, so the MC's job is to enforce equal participation. "Let's pause here for a moment and check in with Chris. We haven't heard from him in a while. Chris, the floor is yours for the next sixty seconds. What's your take on the proceedings?" Finally, the MC needs to check in with everyone at the end of the meeting to ascertain the outcomes, both emotionally and intellectually. "What do you take away from today's meeting, and how do you feel about it?"

CHAPTER SUMMARY

- The online workplace—phone calls, online meetings, and so on—are emotionally stunted, and many problems stem from the inability of humans to get unconscious emotional feedback online, leading to a lack of empathy.

- Our physical and mental experiences are deeply interconnected.

- Our attitudes, emotions, and intentions are mostly unconscious.

- The physical experience opens us up to the mental, rather than the other way around.

- We embody our emotions.

- Our attitudes, emotions, and intentions are profoundly communal and tribal.

- Online business relationships typically have three stages, with a final, wind-down phase.

- In the virtual world, compelling business stories are even more important for engaging your customers, clients, and other audiences.

- Your online presence always needs to meet four criteria: authenticity, clarity, comprehensiveness, and consistency.

THE LACK OF CONTROL

FOR BETTER OR WORSE, YOUR LIFE ONLINE IS PUBLIC

In our real, physical lives, we accept that people close to us change their minds and suffer bad moods—but in the virtual world, we're much less likely to accept this kind of natural inconsistency. We hold others to rigid standards of behavior and are much less forgiving. In virtual space, this double standard is particularly compelling. If you behave badly, it's because you're a troll, and your mother and her mother before you, back a thousand generations. These feelings are not logical, but such is the nature of virtual relationships. Lacking emotional depth, we substitute brittle, intellectual standards. Forgiveness is a word lacking in the digital vocabulary.

This chapter discusses two not-quite-contradictory things. First, it offers some implications of, and necessary responses to, that rigid double standard. And second, it makes a plea that we all take a deep breath and try to relax the double standard just a bit. For the sake of our sanity. For the sake of all those trolls out there. And for the sake of the children, who suffer enormously from online bullying and need our help.

Underlying each of these issues is the fundamental one of control—of what is said about us and others online. We can understand this loss of control whenever our own digital lives are concerned, but we have a hard time extending the same digital flexibility to others.

Our standards are very high online— when it comes to everyone else

If the design team delivers late once, we don't find the behavior understandable, because we're unaware or dismissive of the brutal cold snap that made travel tough and work difficult for a week. The team members' jokes about the bad weather fall flat on the rest of the team, which is based in a warmer climate. It just sounds as if they're suddenly not taking this important project seriously enough.

What does this unconscious double standard do to communication within a team or an organization? Why does this desire for others to play by our rigid rules make it much harder for us to be forgiving of normal human failings in the digital environment? Why do we all become inhuman caricatures of ourselves online?

We need to develop a personal rule book for online communication to save much misunderstanding, miscommunication, and heartache. For ourselves, thinking of the other members of our team, the people in our company, our customers, stakeholders, the public—all the people we might have to interact with—we need to become rigorously consistent or expect that at some point our inconsistencies will be pointed out to us bluntly and unforgivingly.

And for all of us, let's realize that we do have a double standard. Let's remember the Golden Rule. Let's stop judging others quite so harshly. And let's put the human emotions of understanding, acceptance, and charity back into the online world.

Until that golden day arrives, however, if you're going to work and play in the online world, then you need to develop a few online consistency muscles. First, the persona.

What's your online persona?

The need for consistency begins even before you deliberately communicate with others. What's your online persona? It's time to google yourself if you haven't done so recently. Go past the first page, and study thoroughly what's out there, what kind of person the results delineate, and what relationship this bears to your desired persona.

By 2018, "right to be forgotten" rules were gathering adherents in some jurisdictions, but for most of us in most places, the memory of the internet is long.[1] The answer to this problem of the long life of bad news—if it's a problem for you—is not to try to have the record expunged, but rather to drown out the old bad with the good new. Your new persona can find digital immortality by simply being more recent and more plentiful than any old one. So very few of us read past the first page that it's a relatively simple process to scrub your digital persona clean of anything you don't like. Just put out there what you do want to see.

Now take it a step further. Think of yourself as a brand, with a need to be consistent online. Everyone's experience of you needs to be the same, and it needs to be clear, across all the various places that images and information about you can be found. LinkedIn, Twitter, Facebook, Instagram, any other platforms you've inhabited, as well as your website if you have one—what do they say about you? What persona do they present? Is it a consistent, fathomable human being?

Then think, What are your values? You might publish an online values statement to make those clear. People tend to take at face value what you say about yourself, so make your statement in a way that is consistent with who you are and who you want to be seen as.

Now, if your immediate reaction is that a personal brand is something you don't need and don't want, that it's for someone with a much higher profile to worry about, like a celebrity, that's fine; you can skip most of the rest of this chapter. But you put a great deal of effort already into your work and personal lives, dressing the part, acting consistently, behaving according to norms that make sense to you. Why wouldn't you also take control of your online life and make a similar effort?

If you don't, the internet will do it for you. And that's fine, unless its near-perfect memory for those embarrassing spring break pics is something you wish had been forgotten. If transparency, control, and consistency in the various parts of your life are important values for you, then read on.

Creating a personal value statement online

A beautiful example of this kind of transparency, control, and consistency is Chris Palmer, American University's Distinguished Film Producer in Residence.[2] As an environmental activist, he founded American University's Center for Environmental Filmmaking at the School of Communications. He is the president of the MacGillivray Freeman Films Educational Foundation and has produced over three hundred hours of original programming for TV and the IMAX film industry. His films have been broadcast on Animal Planet, the Disney Channel, PBS, and TBS.

His personal mission statement, published on his website, runs to several pages, and he assigns himself seven roles in life. The statement is ambitious, thoughtful, impressive, and, quite frankly, a bit intimidating. Here's the first paragraph of the 2,500-word statement:

> I want to be remembered by my family, friends, and colleagues as a person grounded in decency, simple goodness, infectious vitality, and inspiring enthusiasm; as someone with a lasting and wonderful marriage, a great sense of humor, and a strong work ethic; as a man who made his role and responsibilities as a father and grandfather one of his highest priorities; as a person who committed himself to learning and education and who pursued his goals with passion; and as a man who left the world a better place.[3]

To better understand the purpose and process of this personal mission statement, I asked Palmer what his inspiration was for creating the statement and putting it online. His answer surprised me: "When I was a teenager and in my twenties, I was roiled by moods of despair, overwhelm, rancor, ennui, and confusion. In an effort to find some peace and purpose, it occurred to me to that articulating a vivid description of the life I wanted to lead might help me sort things out and find an inner tranquility. It took me years of effort to finally create a personal mission statement that inspired me when I read it and that I was willing to commit to."

I asked him about people's reaction to the mission statement. He responded, "A few people think I'm excessively serious and even eccentric, but most folks, after reading it, immediately see how it can offer a clarifying vision for one's life and give a person more purpose and meaning."

An online mission statement can change your life

The proof of the concept is in the results, so I asked Palmer what has happened as a result of his creating and publishing a personal mission statement. "It has transformed my life," he said. "I use it to guide my daily activities. Instead of confusion, I have clarity. Instead of feeling overwhelmed, I feel in control. Instead of ennui, I have a purpose."

And what about his *online* life—how has Palmer's online life changed as a result? Palmer said, "People find it online and are intrigued and inspired by it. They write to me for advice and guidance. I give regular talks and presentations on how to live a fulfilling and successful life. About two years ago, I created a new class at American University, where I teach, called Design Your Life for Success. There is high demand to get into the class. One reason for that is because many students worry about how to make sense of their lives and how to lead a life that is meaningful and worthwhile. Rowman & Littlefield published my related book, *Now What, Grad? Your Path to Success After College*. My online life has been greatly enriched by all this work."

If a well-thought-out mission statement seems like a lot of work, it is. But for many people, it beats the alternative, which is to let the rest of the world control the picture of you and develop an opinion of you from online trolling or indifference. Neither picture is liable to be very flattering, after all. And a mission statement is how you can restore the control to your online persona and life that the internet, simply by functioning as a giant recorder for almost everything that happens now, has taken away from you—whether you noticed or not.

Thinking about this work strategically, next you need to develop a platform based on your area of interest and your brand—a platform that like-minded people can respond to and comment on—to help you get your message out. The platform might ultimately take the form of a website, where you have the most control. In the short run, you've probably already created something on Facebook, Twitter, Instagram, LinkedIn, or all those and some other platforms besides.

Focus on your message, not yourself

It's not really about you—if you do it right. It's about your message. That's why people will respond positively and help you develop that persona. They will comment and further your point of view because they care about your idea too. Get the word out, and create ways for the world to join you in the cause you care about.

Even if that cause is simply you because you're thinking about your next job, you still need to get the word out. Don't you think that the first thing a prospective employer will do when thinking about hiring you is google you?

But let's keep it simple. Never mind the website; if that's too much work, you are probably already on Facebook. Think about the difference between a Facebook page for an acquaintance who sends out frequent updates and a page that no one, including the creator, ever visits. What impressions do you form about each person?

You look to the first person for what's going on—and, more importantly, his or her reaction to it. That person becomes a trendsetter for your friends and the person's other friends, and for the internet as a whole—which is to say, the world. If the individual focuses on particular ideas, memes, or issues, you'll get into the habit of looking to this friend's site regularly to understand the trending points of interest.

Of course, there's always the danger that this quasi-public friend will go overboard on an issue and jam your mental inbox—and everyone else's—with too much information about that issue or about themselves. Then you'll quickly tire of the perspective and you may even block or commit online murder: unfriend the person.

The risks of overexposure are real. And underexposure as well. Getting the balance right needs to be part of your plan for your persona and the concepts you want to hold forth on.

Get the balance right

Once you've thought through the ideas you wish to represent and worked through some of these other issues, dig into the process a little deeper. Can people easily find you? When they do find you, what do they see? Do they see a professional website that fits with your personal brand, that makes it easy for them to connect with you, and that continually updates with fresh content? If not, well, you've got some work to do.

And if you hope to be more than a worker bee, then begin to think about developing a voice—a strong point of view on whatever subject you care about. Once you start to develop your point of view, think about press mentions and other search results. Will people searching for you see that you're mentioned in media stories and blog posts related to your field? If not, get to networking.

You get there by creating content and putting it out in some form that makes sense to you and to your field. Focus on the social media you understand best, but make sure you have an active online presence. The alternative is a lack of control of your online life. You'll have to take what's given to you—and you may not like it.

Moreover, you need to take the control even further if you have a passion to make your mark in the world. Create a Facebook fan page, start your blog and contribute regularly to it, post some

YouTube videos in your channel, put your slides online, create a pdf of your press kit—do whatever feels most natural to you to get started. Try to set a regular posting schedule that you can stick with, and then stick with it.

Stuck for ideas? Use your one big idea as a lens and look at the world through it—always. Every moment becomes an opportunity for a new insight, a new data point, a new addition to your bank of stories and wisdom. If everyone's talking about the latest celebrity scandal, see if you can come up with a take that relates back to your big idea. Don't force it, but do look at the headlines with your big idea in mind.

To avoid feeling overwhelmed online, focus

Whatever you're passionate about, that's what you have to find—everywhere. Remember the old saw "To a hammer, everything looks like a nail." Well, you're now a hammer with one or (at most) a few nails. If you're interested in leadership, then every news item becomes a potential blog post about leadership. If you care about technology, then not just every new product announcement, but also every new psychological study about human behavior (for example), becomes grist for the mill. If achievement is your thing, then you need to see its presence or absence everywhere. That's how you keep your expertise alive and fresh. You've got to be scanning the universe constantly.

Finally, the whole point of these efforts is to start a conversation. Once you have some good content to point people to, start engaging with people who are active in your field. Offer guest blog posts to people who write on similar topics. Connect with people on Twitter and other social networks. Answer questions and ask them. Soon enough, people will begin to know you for your ideas and will come to you.

The internally consistent persona is where it all begins

Let's step back a bit and think more deeply about what works in the online world along personal branding lines. What promotes success? What should we strive to look like online? How should we think about our online life? And how do we ultimately control it? Are there any limits, or does anything truly go?

Fortunately, the mental test is simple: we relate to brands the same way we relate to friends and other people—and vice versa. We are drawn to people who exhibit warmth and competence. If we find either one lacking, we respond with suspicion, pity, or disgust.

Brands elicit similar feelings. We want warmth and competence. If we're low on warmth, we get suspicion. If we're low on competence, we get pity. Low on both, we get contempt.

Now, credibility (competence) and trust (warmth) are also prime success factors in communications. Study after study has found that audiences want credibility and trust from their speakers, for example.[4]

The basic outlines of the online persona are thus very human, straightforward, and similar for both people, products, and organizations. According to Susan Fiske and Chris Malone, authors of *The Human Brand: How We Relate to People, Products, and Companie*s, the biggest surprise from their research comes in the area of making mistakes.[5] Counterintuitive as it might seem, the best time to relate to your customers, the authors find, is when you've made a mistake. Provided you respond with authentic contrition and own up to the mistake, you may develop a stronger bond. (The risk, of course, is that because of the fragile nature of trust and connection online, the bond that is broken will be abandoned, not made stronger.)

You can take three steps to build your desired online presence. Think first of all about how you are connecting with your audiences and potential audiences. Where's the warmth? Which of your projected qualities are charming and human?

Second, how are you projecting competence? Do you have a video, a YouTube channel, a blog, an ebook, a published book, a TV or radio show, or some other platform? You need some way to show the world that you know what you're doing.

Third, what are you doing to show authenticity? You don't set out to make mistakes, but you probably will make mistakes in the long run. So you might as well make an acknowledgment of this likelihood part of your long-term narrative. How do you use those mistakes to get closer to your audience?

The human psyche is simple when it comes down to our daily heuristics for determining friendship, brand loyalty, organizational affiliation, and whether we like someone. Ignore human nature at your peril in any of those areas.

In the long run, in sum, keeping track of your digital persona, updating it, and ensuring that it accurately represents what you're trying to achieve are essential parts of taking control of your life and managing your career. All too often, most of us let these important elements slide.

Your online persona is table stakes

Now, all this work I've described is simply the basic hygienic online package you need to create so that the internet—or worse, some enemy, troll, or competitor—doesn't control you. And yet most people will never take the time to think through the issues relating to online personas, branding, and how the online world captures their personalities.

It's a great mistake. Don't fall victim to online passivity. Take control. If you don't take control and disaster does strike, then the only glimpse the rest of the world will ever get of you will be the impression connected to this disaster.

"Nick Morgan" is a common enough name that there are several competitors out there for primacy on Google. My persona dominates simply because I've been far more active online than anyone else who bears my name. But there's a sad twist on the name and an example of how the internet can hijack things you think belong to you.[6] Morgan Nick was a beautiful little girl who disappeared from a Little League baseball game in 1995, apparently kidnapped. She has never been seen again. Her mother worked at turning this tragedy into something positive, creating the Morgan Nick Foundation to help other families whose children have been kidnapped.

In the early days of the internet, Morgan Nick came up every time I googled my own name. Now, Google is more selective and its search engines have improved, so I have to google "Morgan Nick" to find her story anywhere near the top page. Because her name is my name reversed, over the years I've come to imagine an upside-down world where all the Nick Morgans and Morgan Nicks get together, play baseball, and celebrate family. A sort of virtual-name family reunion.

I can afford to take a long view, since my persona is robustly established online. But if you haven't done that work, be prepared to be hijacked by the news one day.

Passivity is dangerous online

You either own and control your persona, or the internet creates and controls one for you. You may or may not like the second version. Certainly, it will not be created with your feelings in mind.

Indeed, most of us have far less control of our digital personas than we realize, simply because we haven't been instrumental in their creation. Typically, a complicated, messy, mostly out-of-date digital legacy is what comes up every time someone googles your name.

Don't think people google you very often? Nowadays, they google your name when you apply for a job, you are asked to give a speech, they meet you for the first time, you try to sell them something, they try to sell you something, you want to go on a date with them, they want to go on a date with you, their teenager wants to date your teenager, and on and on. The point is that googling the names of people we encounter is practically a daily occurrence. You can't escape it.

Preventative maintenance is essential

How do we get ahead of this near-constant googling? Beyond the initial steps I've outlined above, there are three essential steps you should undertake monthly—or at least once a quarter to keep this flood in check.

Start by reviewing all the material that's most immediately under your control. Clean up your own digital tracks—your website, your blog, your social media. Ask yourself, Is there still a consistent theme? Does it represent me in the way I want to be represented? What needs to change? What about me has changed but isn't represented yet?

Then refresh and empty your browser, and google yourself to see what comes up. Is Google saying the right things about you? If not, what can you put out there now that will rise to the top of the Google rankings and supplant whatever's there?

If there's material that doesn't float your boat or market your company, your family, your town, your party—whatever you care about—well, then get to work adding material that does.

Plan to refresh your brand regularly, with expert help. The cobbler's children never have any shoes, or so the saying goes. And most people are busy doing whatever it is that is their main work. This important housecleaning job won't get done if you don't build it into your schedule. For any kind of control of your online life, you should be refreshing your brand at minimum once a year. For many fields of expertise, more often than that will be necessary. And get expert help, because you won't do it as well as someone with a little bit of distance will.

You are what shows up about you on the web, just as much as you are yourself in real life. In fact, for most people you interact with, your digital persona is more important than your face-to-face reality.

What does your persona say about you right now? Remember the double standard—the human tendency to judge other people more harshly than we judge ourselves—and all those other people with your name. Shape your own story online, lest you be shaped.

Understand the benefits and perils of search engine optimization

If you've hung on this far in the chapter, it's probably because you want to be more than merely perceived as consistent and somewhat au courant online. You want to be noticed. Of course, once you're noticed, then the importance of all the aforementioned work increases exponentially, because the trolls will be out with their clubs for you, looking for inconsistencies and hypocrisies.

So do the work first. But let's say you have done it and now you want to get noticed online. What to do next? First, the bad news. There are no shortcuts to getting noticed online. It's not about search engine optimization (SEO) or enjoying the sheer luck of going viral or some other voodoo. All that stuff changes so fast that if you chase it, you'll be chasing a chimera forever.

What does it take to get noticed? You must build a community, that is, a community of people who have similar interests and who come to you as one locus of the discussion that interests them. This community is what insulates and protects you from the haters, the trolls, and the people looking to feed off your misery. If you have a strong-enough community, it will come to your aid when you most need it, when you're under attack from some weird, angry troll.

You build a community with content and issue marketing. The details of all the steps involved in such marketing lie outside the scope of this book. Whole books have been written on the subject, and none better than David Meerman Scott's *New Rules of Marketing and PR*, a perennial best seller now in its sixth edition.[7] Scott is an expert on the subject, and a quick internet search of his name will yield a good deal of free insight as well as his many books on the subject.

In brief, to create buzz today, you first need dedication to an area of content you are passionate about and have some expertise in. Then, when you put that content out there in the social media stream where the world will see it, Google will rank it and people will start to cluster around you to discuss it.

The test of sincerity in that kind of marketing is time and depth. We tend to believe experts who have spent the hours figuring out the issues in their field and have dug deep enough that they've uncovered some convincing answers. Initial attention and then the memories it takes in each human brain to get the world to continue to pay attention are not created instantly; they need time to develop.

SEO comes from time and passion for a topic

What sort of content helps focus that attention and create those memories? People have two mental processes to create memories. Either they remember things verbatim or they remember the gist.[8] We're more likely to remember verbatim phrases if they are clever, and rhyme or repeat in some way. We remember the gist better if it has a strong emotional component. "If the glove does not fit, you must acquit." At least that's how I remember the phrase developed by the brilliant lawyer Johnnie Cochran to defend his client O. J. Simpson.

Repetition is key, as is simplicity. And pictures don't serve for a thousand words. Pictures need to be simple and fit into people's predetermined categories to be remembered well: puppies, kittens, cute small furry things. Words that create pictures in your mind are as good as—if not better than—pictures. But the internet likes pictures more and more, so you want to think about the visual representation of your ideas early and often. For more on this memory-making process, check neuroscientist Carmen Simon's excellent book *Impossible to Ignore: Creating Memorable Content to Influence Decisions.*[9]

Get started with your online story

Here are five questions that I've found over the years help people get started developing their online brand and persona.

What do I stand for, and who is in my community? The first half of this question seems harder and more cosmic than the latter half, so start with the latter if it's easier. Imagine you had the single perfect community member in front of you. Who would that be? And then, what are the general demographics of your tribe—the people you want to address?

Once you clarify who your community is, then figuring out what you might say to them comes next with surprising ease. OK, the job's not done yet, but you have made a great start.

What really ticks me off? Rants are great ways to reveal values and positions. Asking yourself what you hate is not about going dark or negative, but is rather about finding the outlines of the light that you're seeking. Rants are liberating, too. In every sphere of modern life except the political, we spend a good deal of time making nice, concealing our true feelings, and getting along with people we occasionally want to string up. So a rant is just healthy for the system.

What will the world look like if I'm able to change it? Looking ahead and assuming success, you get to play in an online world that's at least partly your creation. It's fun, and it's liberating, too, to imagine a world cured of the ills you perceive and made better in the ways that matter to you. Get started describing that world.

What are three nonnegotiable values I live by? What am I willing to compromise on? Understanding the difference between your must-haves and nice-to-haves is a key way of delineating your values and your ideas. These vary enormously from person to person and system to system, so getting clear on the essentials and the frills takes you a long way down the road to an idea.

What's the problem my community has for which my expertise or passion is the solution? This is the sand in the passion oyster—

the issues that people turn to you for, time and again. It is the pain point that you can diagnose instantly and always see the way forward from. If you're in an organization, it's the problem that the rest of the team always calls on you for. Do they turn to you for people advice, systems issues, or procedural problems? Your expertise shows up naturally at certain moments and for certain needs. Focus on those needs, and you'll know the way forward.

Control of your online persona and life is both a necessity and a discipline for any of us who have an online life. And if you don't think you do, think again. You're probably listed on at least several websites, not to mention Facebook and other social media. It's time to control your virtual presence.

I close this chapter with a return to the topic I raised at the beginning: a plea to end the double standard all too many of us have when it comes to online behavior and forgiveness. "Judge not, lest ye be judged" is a biblical dictum that is the inverse of the Golden Rule, and both admonitions should have huge currency on the internet. We need to reclaim our lost humanity on the web. We need to restore the emotions that all too many of the digital conveniences of the modern world have silently and unthinkingly taken away. We don't notice their loss until someone lashes out at us in a cold, hostile, or harsh way and we wonder, "What has happened to humanity? People never used to be like that!" What we really mean is that the online world has hurt us emotionally and it's time to begin the work, every day and globally, of putting the emotions back into our online tribes, worlds, and communities. We need to act with charity, with kindness, with forbearance, and with an understanding of our shared humanity—and we want everyone else to act that way toward us as well. It takes us all, working together, to achieve anything like that.

Let's get started. Let's agree to be truly consistent about ourselves and toward others and to remember the Golden Rule.

Practical fix

The published value statement

Every team that works together in the virtual space needs to spend some time at the beginning of the relationship establishing its jointly held values—and a process for voicing and resolving problems when those values are violated. Some examples of these value statements exist in work teams in the real world, but they are even more important in the virtual space, both for the work the team must do to establish them jointly and for the process of resolving value violations.

Use these questions to develop a value statement, either a personal one or a team one, that you publish online in a place that is appropriate for your or your team's aims.

> What do I (we) stand for, and who is in my (our) community?
>
> What do I (we) love, and what do I (we) hate?
>
> What are my (our) nonnegotiable values?
>
> What's the problem I'm (we're) solving?
>
> And the details, such as these questions: What's the best way to communicate with me (us), how should people raise issues, what is my (our) process for resolving them, and how long do we anticipate working on the problem we're getting together for?

CHAPTER SUMMARY

- We often forgive inconsistency with people we know well face-to-face, but we rarely forgive inconsistent online behavior.

- To weather the resulting online storms, we need to develop an online persona.

- A personal online mission statement is a good place to start.

- Begin by focusing your voice on a particular issue, passion, or idea.

- If you haven't done so already, check your current online persona.

- And then make it a regular practice to review your persona at least quarterly.

- Once you've gotten behind an issue and started to develop a persona, begin publishing, find your community, and—most of all—embrace online consistency.

- The best SEO is to speak volubly online about your passion; consistency and passion count because they are measures of authenticity.

- And remember to forgive others as you would be forgiven.

THE LACK OF EMOTION

CAN YOU MAKE ME CARE?

Have you ever put a conference call on mute while talking to a colleague at your desk or while doing the dishes or checking Facebook? Then why do *you* keep booking hour-long conference calls and expecting people to stay focused the whole time? When we can't see each other, we can't rely on unconscious cues to let us know when the group is drifting and everyone needs a break. Virtual communication requires us to make an extra effort to be connected in human ways to our colleagues and to think through when and how we're reaching people—is this email arriving right before my colleague is sitting down to dinner?—because it doesn't happen naturally in the virtual space.

One of the cardinal virtues of email and its descendant, texting, was supposed to be that it was asynchronous, meaning I could send you my note in the middle of night when I was unable to sleep, and you could read it comfortably over your morning coffee. But mobile phones and being always-connected means that, for most people most of the time, we are constantly being pinged by texts and emails and other forms of interruptions that demand a quick response. I've also noted that whereas in the past you could respond to an email, say, in a few days and still be considered polite, now you'll get a follow-up email a few hours later if you don't respond almost immediately.

The failure to connect in real human terms goes both ways, and fundamentally, it comes from a lack of emotion. Research shows that most of us have trouble judging emotional tone in written communications.[1] Being an effective, connected communicator means making an extra effort to try to understand where your colleagues are coming from. For example, you might begin the conference call with a check-in that allows everyone a minute to talk about his or her immediate state of mind and working conditions. In this chapter, we'll explore the missing element of virtual connection—the lack of emotion—and how to reestablish it in ongoing team communications as well as in onetime virtual engagements.

The missing cues make online communicating difficult

For the human who craves real connection—and that's most of us—virtual communicating is deeply unpleasant. Why? The normal cues that we get in face-to-face communications are largely missing. The result is an emotional void. Let's look a little deeper at why the two kinds of communication are so different.

Every face-to-face communication is two simultaneous conversations: the content (what you say) and the body language (how you say it).[2] Both these conversations are essential to human communication, but they are very different. The content is the stuff of everyday chitchat, high-level planning, offers of employment and marriage, negotiations to end wars, and secret deals to share marketplaces around the world. The second conversation is far simpler and far more important in one sense: if the two conversations are not aligned, then the second one always trumps the first. We've all had the experience of saying one thing and meaning another. Sometimes, we want to convey something else, and other times, we want to hide something.

Body language trumps content because body language is concerned with some very basic questions about our individual survival and the survival of the species. We ask ourselves, Is this person a threat? Then, if this person is not a threat, is he or she more or less powerful than me? Next, can I reproduce with this person? Then, can he or she reproduce with me? And finally, have I seen this person or pattern before, or is it new?

These are not questions that we vocalize explicitly, for the most part. Most often, we're not even conscious of them; they are posed and answered by our unconscious minds to other unconscious minds and back again. But take these questions away, and suddenly our interest in the conversation becomes minimal to nonexistent.

Minimal to nonexistent—and considerably more savage than it would otherwise be. When you remove the second conversation—the body language—you remove the ability to experience the normal restraints of human connection.

That's what happens in the virtual world. There is an emotional void, which is precisely the problem. The virtual world is inherently uninteresting because it takes survival out of the equation. It takes human interest out of the equation. And it takes emotion—the basis of pattern recognition—out of the equation. What's left no longer engages our deep connections with other people. A virtual conversation is not important to our unconscious minds (survival), it's not engaging (human interest), and it's not moving (emotion).

Fill the emotional void

And taking these emotions out of the natural human connection means that things get dark fast. We either get bored, or we get nasty. Or both.

Let's look at the result by putting ourselves in a common scenario. It's Monday morning. It's time for the usual team conference call. You have them every Monday morning at 10:00 Eastern Standard Time because that's 3:00 p.m. (midafternoon) for the UK team, midmorning for the New York team, and not too early for the California contingent. Actually, the 7:00 a.m. start was fine for Jake back when he was the only member of the team on the West Coast, because he drove into the office every weekday morning at 6:00 a.m. to miss most of the notorious Los Angeles traffic. And as other teammates were added in LA, they were socialized to fit Jake's—and the rest of the team's—schedule. Now Jake has gone, but no one has bothered to change the habit, and the time has remained the same.

You're the moderator and you start the call promptly at 10:00 a.m. from the New York office. The UK team is late signing on because of a work lunch that had something to do with a new group being added there. You knew this and decided to go ahead because you wanted to introduce the new marketing concept that is going to be so important for selling the new gadget and that everyone needs to understand. The UK team members were instrumental in developing the slide deck, so you presumed that they could catch up easily enough.

You sign on to the company conference line, but because of a screwup, you have to change the invite to a Webex conference bridge. This change delays things a bit more because you have to send out the instructions to everyone via email. Naturally, not everyone picks up the email in time; a few stragglers never do find out, and so the ultimate roll call is incomplete.

But you finally get the call going and ask if everyone has the slide deck. A few people in LA, and even one or two in the New York office, don't seem to have gotten the memo. There goes another seven minutes sorting that out.

Finally, everyone has the deck, and maybe it was even a good thing that the meeting started late because the UK team has rolled in from lunch at last and is in good spirits. The first thing one of them says is that the first word on the first slide is misspelled.

Virtual criticism stings more than in-person criticism

You bridle. You're a bit of perfectionist, and anyway, you want this rollout to go well and you want people to be impressed. If they're obsessing about typos—heck, if they're even looking for typos—you're going to be in trouble.

They may be saying it with a smile, but you can't see the smile.

"What do you mean?" you ask. "I've spell-checked this thing a dozen times. Where?"

Ian chuckles. "Color. C-o-l-o-u-r."

Oh, he's making a joke about English versus American spelling. Great. Funny. The future of the company is at stake, and he's debating Noah Webster's attempts to modernize English spelling for Americans in the nineteenth century.

"Thanks, Ian," you say. "Go back to sleep." You wince. The comment just slipped out, but Ian will take it as a reference to the time he fell asleep in a meeting in the United States, thanks to jet lag, one of the last face-to-face meetings the team could afford to have, a couple of years ago. People have been reminding him of it ever since, and it's not really a joke. The president of the company dropped by just at the wrong moment, and Ian's career chances took a sudden nosedive.

Because you can't see each other, you can't put a little psychic salve on the situation by smiling to show that you didn't mean it.

Indeed, things go ominously quiet from the UK end.

You pause and take a deep breath. Maybe it's a good time to ask all the team members what they think? No, it's too early. You need to get back on track and finish the slide deck. You don't even know if everyone has had a chance to look at the thing, so it's essential that you go through it to get everyone at the same level.

But where are they in their attention levels and engagement? Recent studies show that on a typical conference call, over 60 percent of the supposed participants are doing email, other work, going to the bathroom, shopping, exercising, or eating—or even taking another call.[3]

It's not a pretty picture. Over 80 percent of teams and 90 percent of projects have at least one team member not physically in the same location as the other workers. The number of workers who work from home at least one day a week has increased by 79 percent from 2005 to 2012.[4]

It's a virtually isolated world

We are experiencing an epidemic of emotional isolation. But the issue is not simply that we can't see each other because we're not in the same physical place. If that were all there were to it, then Skype and Google Hangouts would solve all our virtual isolation issues.

We're only beginning to understand the full extent of how our unconscious minds gather information about the world around us and, specifically, the people around us. In the interests of efficiency and through the historical accident of invention, we've adopted a system of digital communication that is deeply unsatisfying for us humans, because it doesn't allow us to gather and exchange the information that we want in the way that we're used to.

But even more important, our digital communication prevents us from connecting emotionally with our fellow humans. That (largely) unconscious emotional connection is a key aspect of our human information gathering and sharing system. Indeed, it's hardwired in us. Without it, the information is far poorer, far less generous, and far more often misunderstood. In fact, it's usually incoherent, as we'll see.

So why is emotional connection so important to communications? Why do virtual communications almost completely eliminate it, leading to all the bad behavior we see in the virtual world? And what other problems does the absence of emotion cause in the human exchange of information?

Why does human emotional connection matter so much?

As an acting student, I had the privilege of witnessing a then-well-known Broadway actor demonstrate his facility with emotions. Actors think of themselves as expert in emotions; it's their job, in one sense, to be able to conjure up emotions with ease. They are professionally emotional, if you will. The subject had turned to that gold standard of acting emotions, the crying scene. We students were nervously admitting that we found it hard to cry on command, for a particular scene or situation.

We wondered if we would be up to it when the need came along. The actor didn't say anything in response. He simply turned his back for a few moments and then turned around again—with tears streaming down his face.

It was a showy way of making his point. He wanted us to see that he had a wide range of emotions ready at a moment's notice, and he wanted us to understand that it was our job to prepare the same (roughly speaking) set of emotions for instant recall.

He produced that emotion from one of the two sources of connection that humans possess. The first, but less powerful source, is our imagination—his method, in fact. He conjured up in his mind a memory of grief—a moment when he had been sad—and let the tears flow accordingly.

For years, researchers thought that imagination was the primary source of human emotional connection. Because we have experienced moments of joy, sorrow, excitement, and sadness, when we see one of those emotions in someone else, we compare, in effect, our memory of the emotion with what we're seeing, match it up, and react accordingly. Human connection, under this theory, is essentially a memory-retrieval exercise.

But the second and more powerful source of emotional connection is the more direct one. It turns out that emotional connection is how we're hardwired as humans. And removing that natural, easy, unconscious emotional data stream, therefore, as virtual communication does surprisingly well, is particularly crippling.

How does this second source of emotional connection work?

We can't help trying to connect with one another

A team of Italian researchers was studying the basic workings of the brain, using monkeys as subjects, in the 1990s.[5] The researchers were interested in several aspects of the brain, and as they worked with the monkeys, the scientists gave out peanuts—a snack the monkeys loved—as rewards for good behavior. The peanuts caused the monkeys' pleasure circuits to light up, as the machines they were hooked up to showed.

One researcher ate a peanut himself rather than give it to the monkey, which could see both the offending researcher and the peanut. Rather than experiencing anger, as you might expect, the monkey apparently felt pleasure: the pleasure circuits of the animal's brain lit up just as if the monkey had received the peanut itself.

This astonishing result led to much more research. In the end, the team discovered that when we (and monkeys) see someone else experience an emotion, that same emotion fires in our heads—thanks to what the team called *mirror neurons*. The far more powerful and important source of empathy, then, is these mirror neurons. Our brains themselves produce in our own heads the same emotions that we witness in people around us. A set of clues coming to us in the visual and wider sensory field, and in the tone of voice of the people near us, causes us to mirror excitement, anger, joy, or terror back to the people who are experiencing it themselves.

Emotional connection is part of our wiring

This is what human connection really is: the hard wiring in our brains forces us to feel the same emotion that other people around us feel. We crave this emotional connection because we're hardwired to experience it, and we suffer when it's removed. In the virtual space, mirror neurons don't fire, because they don't get the information they need to do so.

How does this failure happen? Take away the visual field, restrict the tonal field, and you hugely hamper connection.

You're back to relying on the uncertain activity of the imagination. Most of us are more like acting students in this regard than that Broadway star. We're a bit tentative when it comes to the imaginary projection into other people's emotions; sometimes we get it wrong. Sometimes we imagine the wrong emotion or the wrong intensity. And sometimes we don't bother at all.

What else happens when emotional connection is restricted? Oddly enough, in addition to behaving badly toward others, we lose the ability to make decisions—especially group decisions—as readily as before. Trying to establish the prevailing mood of the participants in a virtual meeting, in short, can become extremely problematic. The purpose of a virtual meeting is hard to pin down because, stripped down to the basics, decision making is about sharing emotions. Emotions allow us a way of weighing the relative importance of all the inputs involved. If you and your partner are trying to decide on a new floor in the kitchen, for example, emotions make the decision possible. You and your partner mirror each other, share emotions, and find out how important various aspects of the decisions are. You like the tile, but that reminds your partner of a childhood kitchen— and that's a bad thing. Or, it's a good thing. Mirror neurons help you determine the difference. In the end, you go with the wood floor because it reminds both of you of that wonderful Airbnb place you stayed at six months ago. You just loved the rustic feel and the open, airy sense of space the kitchen had.

Humans base decisions on emotions

Most of the decisions we make are made like that flooring decision. Or they're made even faster, with less reflection, and with an even greater reliance on emotions (and mirror neurons). Do you take a different route to work to miss the traffic? Do you decide to go out to the movies? Do you say yes to your boss when he or she offers you that new project (more responsibility, more work, but do it well, and you might get a raise)?

You can draw a straight line from emotions to decision making to mirror neurons. These three elements are essential to a coherent life.

Neuroscientists point to a landmark case in their field. A man had suffered a stroke that damaged the hippocampus. This part of the brain has an essential role in handling emotions. The man could no longer make decisions about anything; he lived in an agony of indecision and immobility, frozen in his inability to act. Why? He had no basis for choice.[6] No emotions tugged at him to say, choose this way, because it will make your spouse happy. Or, choose that one, because it will make your boss respect you.

And here's the rub for the virtual world. Without emotion, communications become, if not impossible, at least far more difficult. People with autism experience something very like this. It's what I experienced for a few months when I was seventeen, as I described in my previous book *Power Cues*.[7] A brain injury had temporarily disabled my unconscious ability to read other people's emotions in the same instant way that most humans can.

Without human connection via unconscious emotions, we live in a void

And from my experience with a brain injury, I can tell you that when you take away the emotional connection, not only does it become difficult to understand other people, but the whole project of life seems less interesting, less engaging, and less important. While my brain recovered, I drifted, unable to take my normal interest in the things going on around me and my seventeen-year-old (damaged) brain.

Mirror neurons enable us to understand and entertain another person's point of view or another person's pain. Without mirror neurons, negotiating successfully with other people is more difficult, if not impossible, because it's hard to engage in sympathetically understanding the other party's emotions. You can't decide how important one bargaining chip or another is. You can't tell whether the other side is bluffing. You can't gauge where everybody is on the issues.

That's the virtual world. What's missing is the human emotional connection. Taking it out makes communication infinitely more difficult.

And we can get a little more specific. Some emotions—namely, the most basic ones, such as anxiety, fear, happiness, and joy—are more contagious than others. Take away the empathy, and these emotions are the first to fall. The reasons most likely have to do with the basic hardwired questions we humans ask ourselves, questions that are highly dependent on our unconscious minds, a quick read, and empathy.

What happens in the virtual world when you make experiencing these basic emotions—and sharing them—more difficult? Anxiety and fear top the list of emotions that get lost. And you might think that's a good thing. But negative emotions exist to keep us out of trouble and, once we're in trouble, to help us escape it as fast as possible. Dull the fight-or-flight response, and you dull your survival abilities. That's not helpful in organizational life or anywhere else.

Next up are happiness and joy, with the triggers of laughter and smiling. Take those out, and life and work become a lot less interesting and a lot less fun.

Finally, there's attraction. Take out love and friendship, and you have a much harder time getting anything done.

Without the motivating power of the voice, what's left?

But it's not only the visual field that's impaired in the virtual world. Surprisingly, what we hear suffers as well.

One of the most extraordinary abilities we humans possess is one that we rarely think about consciously. I would even wager that this moment may be the first time you've ever thought about the following strange fact. We humans can instantly recognize—without any apparent effort—hundreds of individual human voices.[8]

Our loved ones, our friends and colleagues, famous people, politicians, the corner grocer—we can conjure up the identity of the speaker in an instant. We do no conscious work, except in the rare instance when we have to think about the voice for a moment longer because your mother's voice and your aunt Sally's sound so much alike on the phone. I'll get back to that in a moment.

That rapid recognition comes from our unconscious mind's uncanny ability to analyze the aural fingerprint of the voice. The human voice is a mixture of the pitch it is speaking at and the overtones and undertones at thirds, fifths, octaves, and so on, above and below the actual pitch. If you recorded a voice on an oscilloscope, it would look like a fuzzy line going up and down—like a recording of ground vibrations on a seismograph.

Researchers used to believe that those undertones and overtones were random—just part of the unique sound of your voice or my voice or Winston Churchill's. But it turns out that they are far more important than that, especially in two ways.

First, the undertones in particular convey emotions. So remove the undertones, and you make human conversation much less interesting. And remember the man who could no longer make decisions when a stroke removed his ability to process emotions? Removing the undertones from the human voice makes it much harder to reach decisions.[9]

You can't lead people over the telephone

Besides hindering decision making, removing undertones from human speech has other effects. In fact, those undertones also allow people to choose their leaders. When you get a group of people together in a room, one of the first things they do is unconsciously elect a leader. It takes no more than fifteen minutes, and—incredibly—we elect a leader and signal our followership by matching our undertones to those of the leader whom we've elected.

Take away the undertones, and we take away the innate ability to create a leader, an authority, and followers. And, of course, the titular leader can't assume the assigned chores with any real, unconscious power, because the clues are all missing.

But that's precisely what virtual communication does; it prevents us from selecting a leader or leading. To create the telephone in the early days, engineers figured out how to compress the human voice (and still make it comprehensible) by removing the undertones and overtones beyond a basic range of pitches. The compression was essential in the early days to convey the voice (roughly intact, as far as anyone knew) over those primitive copper wires.

Now we have fiber optics and the ability to convey vast amounts of information virtually, but guess what? We still compress the voice. Because, why decompress it? It would take up too much bandwidth. There's never been a good time to suddenly make something as basic as the voice much more costly in information terms to convey across the wired and wireless networks that span the world.

The result is that the virtual world removes not only the emotional components that create connection but also the unconscious signals that create leaders, followers, and decisions. It's amazing that we can get anything done at all in the virtual sphere.

As I hope you're now beginning to see, the virtual space we've created is uniquely set up to make it difficult for us to conduct our human business in the way that we've done for thousands of years. We think we've created something convenient, cost-effective, and efficient. Instead, we've created something that is stultifying, expensive in terms of emotions and decision making, and wildly inefficient.

As emotion goes, so goes communication

I was leading a group of special ops officers in body-language training. These were some of the toughest dudes on the planet—big, trained in the martial arts and other kinds of hand-to-hand combat, and ready to lead. To lead them, and for the purposes of the training, I quickly noted that I had to step up my confidence through posture and voice or risk becoming discounted by this group as a wimp.

I found myself standing taller, puffing out my chest, and pushing my voice into a lower register in a (probably vain) attempt to make myself a bigger, badder dude than I really was. The team was all men, and there was an air of both camaraderie and jockeying for top dog. I found the interactions fascinating to watch—and couldn't help joining in—until it became clear that I was never going to be the alpha male in this group.

I had to settle for somewhere in the middle of the pack. Now I know, thanks to our understanding of mirror neurons, that my best move would have been to observe the behavior and then subtly mirror it, without trying to be the number one male in the room. Just joining the pack, on some days, is good enough. And my lower voice helped a little, but probably not as much as I wanted it to, because I had almost undoubtedly pushed it too low to maximize my authority and become the leader.

Just joining the pack is good enough. And, in fact, essential. And yet, virtual communications robs us of this aspect of the relationship and this kind of connection. Because that's what tribal belonging is—emotional connection on a group scale.

Online communication often fails, but you can help ameliorate it

Are there ways to improve the experience of connection in virtual situations? Can we buck the communications tide and reverse the downward spiral of misunderstanding, boredom, and ineffectiveness? Cogito Corporation, a spinoff of MIT's media lab, is working on precisely that question.[10] Practically, what can we do to restore some of the connection that the virtual world takes out?

There are a couple of ways to improve the dismal experience of audioconferences, webinars, and even "telepresence rooms" and other forms of visual virtual connection. We have a whole set of unconscious behaviors that help regulate the flow of ordinary conversation. We make eye contact, we nod, we lean forward, we wave our hands—and we do all these things without being aware of them, and without being aware of others doing them too. But these behaviors are extraordinarily helpful in making conversation seem smooth, avoiding endless interruptions, and allowing everyone a chance to feel heard.

Without those unconscious clues, you need to develop an equivalent set of conscious ones. You need to become exceedingly conscious about taking turns and allowing others to do so. People signal each other, for example, in ordinary conversation when they are nearly ready to stop talking. In effect, they're telling the other person, "Almost done. Get ready, because it's almost your turn."

Lacking that visual clue, you might put it into your conversation consciously. "I'm almost done here, so let me turn the conversation over to you after one more comment." Something like that. It might seem hopelessly artificial, but the alternative is something we've all suffered through—the endless interruptions, apologies for interruptions, and awkward silences that make up a team meeting on the phone.

Substitute conscious communication cues for the missing unconscious ones

Similarly, you can help determine the pacing and give-and-take of a virtual conversation with deliberate clues about the length of turns and the handoffs. "Let's each take about one minute to comment on this point that Geoff has raised, going around the team in order by time zone. Jane, do you want to start?"

Again, that sort of mediating may seem like hard work, but the alternative is far more irritating for everyone. And exhausting. People regularly report on the creative ways they have come up with to tune out audioconferences, from personal grooming to exercising to even flipping back and forth between more than one conversation.

Second, the emotions we can convey effortlessly when we are face-to-face can to a certain extent be added back into a virtual conversation by consciously varying the pitch and pacing of your voice. We signal excitement (and stress) by speaking faster and raising our pitch. By slowing down and lowering your pitch, you can indicate the opposite—authority and calm. You can do this consciously, with some effort and a good deal of practice. Learning to put back in the emotions that the virtual world strips out of our communications is an essential survival skill in the twenty-first century.

Practical fix

The virtual temperature check

Research shows that most of us have trouble judging tone in written communications or any form of virtual communication, even phone calls. Being an effective, empathetic communicator means making an extra effort to understand where your colleagues are coming from. For your team, create a simple three-stage "temperature" check you use to begin each virtual communication. Green could mean "good, ready to go." Yellow, "I'm having a crappy day and need to be cut a little slack." And red could mean "I'm close to a meltdown and should be approached with extreme care."

How would this checkup work on your weekly team call? First of all, you need agreement on the importance of starting on time. Tardiness is a problem in face-to-face meetings, too, but at least in-person chitchat while you wait is easier. On a conference call, without the nonverbal cues, it's very difficult to make unplanned, casual conversation as relaxed and natural as it should be. So keep it to a minimum by enforcing precise starting times.

Once everyone has joined in, the convener of the meeting should immediately ask for a temperature check-in around the group. Call each name, and get a clear response. Green indicates a participant who's in good spirits, well-rested, ready to participate and pay full attention with no significant stressors pulling the person away. Yellow means that all is not right in this person's world—perhaps the individual is facing a significant deadline or issues from outside work, like a sick child, that are making life more difficult at the moment. And finally, red means that the person is having a day from hell—significant problems either at work or at home—and needs to be dealt with as gently as possible or should be excused entirely.

The color responses then should guide you, as the moderator, to offer the participants the chance to say more about their particular state of mind or to keep their issues off the table. You'd say something like, "Laura, you reported in as yellow. Do you want to mention what is causing you to have a less-than-stellar day?" Red responses should provoke an offer to be excused from the meeting—if humanly possible—and be assisted as needed. And green responses should allow the moderator to ask about any good news to share.

The whole exchange should only take a couple of minutes and will give the virtual participants a chance to state their emotional temperature—precisely the sort of simple check that would easily and naturally be carried out by the unconscious mind in face-to-face meetings. This kind of analysis can also be charted over time if recorded to provide valuable data about the emotional attitudes of workers and their fluctuations as the work year progresses.

CHAPTER SUMMARY

- We humans crave emotional connection, but the virtual world can't easily provide it.

- The emotional connections in the virtual world—if they exist at all—are more fragile and prone to error.

- Mirror neurons enable us to connect emotionally in person, but the mirroring process doesn't work online.

- Without these emotional tools, we fail to connect—to communicate the emotions we need for connections—and to make decisions.

- Leadership becomes much harder with only virtual communication tools.

- We need to replace the unconscious connection tools with virtual conscious ones.

THE LACK OF CONNECTION AND COMMITMENT

ANYONE HERE FROM DUBUQUE?

How can we build connection—and make it last—online? We humans crave commitment, a happy state that is increasingly rare online. In this chapter, I'll talk about the difficulties inherent in online connection and commitment—and what to do about them.

Ultimately, whether you're communicating face-to-face or virtually, you want to know that you've made the connection, sealed the deal, gotten the commitment. But in the virtual world, you have fewer ways to judge the reality of the commitment than in the real world. Trust is more fragile, and people are more inclined to kick the tires—with suspicion—in the digital world. How do you know what you're getting?

In the virtual world, you can't accomplish the same kind of gut check that leads to a handshake deal in the real world. So maybe you decide to trust reluctantly and provisionally, or maybe not. It's much harder to get closure in the virtual world, especially when the stakes are higher than, say, buying a paper-back book on Amazon.

We need to learn a new mode of transparent behavior with our clients and customers, our teams, and our more distant colleagues to build a new kind of virtual engagement, one that leads to commitment in the end. We further need to open the door for approaches that *combine* both the virtual and the physical in our engagements. Though still in its infancy, the research shows that the combination can become a powerful way to keep people engaged.

Ultimately, as I argued in the last chapter, people crave human emotional connection—in everything. We are social beings. At the end of all our efforts to insulate and isolate ourselves from human pain, inconsistency, and abandonment, we always come back for more. And yet virtual connections are more fragile and less satisfying than in-person ones. Unconsciously, we want our virtual connections to feel the same as our in-person ones—just as real, just as satisfying, just as emotionally compelling—but they can't fill that need. The research suggests that as virtual working relationships have increased, employee engagement has gone down, job dissatisfaction has increased, and turnover has risen.[1]

The virtual working world is not working.

The minimum personal relationship is not enough for us

When you work in the same office with someone five days a week, you naturally build up at least a minimal personal relationship. That relationship helps cement your connection to your workplace, your team, and your organization. Over a long period, you feel committed to the other people in your office, absent any serious conflicts. When you work on a virtual team, those watercooler or coffeepot opportunities for casual chat are largely gone.

Why do we feel the lack of that kind of connection and commitment so deeply? Why is it so important to add those personal connections back in to virtual communications if we can? How can you take advantage of recent research along those lines? How can you become a strong virtual connector? Let's explore.

Let's get to the silver lining right away. The majority of companies today use some kind of social networking tools to connect their employees, according to a McKinsey & Company survey.[2] The growing use of these kinds of tools provided researcher Lynn Wu of Wharton with a perfect opportunity to study how they impact the bottom line for companies and for individual employees. After all, social networking has become ubiquitous in our daily lives, and we're all familiar with the consequences— the way we can connect with far-flung friends and family, and the way we can sit in the same room with a friend and stare at our phones. Wu wondered, how would social networking tools affect the results-oriented world of work?

The results of her research were surprising.[3] Wu chose to study consultants so that she could understand how social networking affected an individual's bottom-line results, in the form of billable revenue. Her first finding was that using social networks helped these consultants access more-diverse sources of information and that this "information diversity" paid off in increased billable revenue. So, there was a direct bottom-line boost, for the individual, from connecting with more people within the organization.

Wu's second major finding was even more revealing. Her research took her through the recession of 2009, when millions of people in many industries lost their jobs. She found that the *more* that individuals used social words in their chats with colleagues, like "coffee," "lunch," or "football," the *less likely* they were to be laid off. In fact, using social words was a better predictor of a person's keeping a job than were more-objective measures, like billable revenue.

Wu discussed the implications of her research in an interview: "I'm not saying that people should necessarily just stop working and [use social media] all the time. But perhaps there's a value that social communication can provide that we don't see. Perhaps this person is a really good team player, and people really enjoy working with this person. Maybe he did not bill directly, but he enabled his coworkers or his colleagues to do a better job."[4]

In other words, the use of those social words in communications with colleagues might be a signal of efforts to build strong connections that are helping a team get more work done. That's encouraging for managers; watercooler chat, whether it takes place in the physical or the virtual world, can be seen as an indicator, at least, of the desire for strong collaborative relationships on a team.

For individuals, though, the implications of Wu's research are even clearer: it pays to schmooze, even through the weaker connections of the online world. "Obviously you want to do a good job," Wu explained. "But you also should worry about intangible communication or other things you have to do at work to make it more likely that you'll be keeping your job or maybe promoted or improve your career outcome."

Connection and job security are closely tied

Wu also warned that social networking tools have a dark side. Because they enable people to quickly amass social capital, they can also create a divide between the digital-relationship haves and have-nots. If you lack the social capital to make connections easily on your team, perhaps because you're a remote worker and the rest of the team works together face-to-face, you could find yourself falling farther and farther behind. Wu's research proves that it pays to be conscious of your social capital and to make a point of connecting socially with your colleagues—if you want to keep your job.

But given how important these online tools are becoming, how can we refine them to make them more than the crude instruments for distraction that—all too often—they can be now? How can we give them the weight they apparently deserve—and develop for ourselves the connection and commitment we all crave?

First of all, make these tools real. Don't use social networking as the online equivalent of sucking up to your boss. You'll get a lot more emotional satisfaction and real connection if you make the online and the face-to-face continua of one another. The old saying "On the internet, no one knows that you're a dog" was true enough. But today, we've learned that it's important for authenticity and self-consistency to be real online.

Second, use social networking to expand your sphere of competence. If you've done the work in the previous chapters to figure out who you are and what you stand for online, then you're ready to put your passion to work creating an outsized reputation in the field that matters to you. Become the go-to person in your organization for something that matters to you and that you can go the distance on.

Third, use online networking to be vulnerable. Few online moves work better than vulnerability to garner support and offers of help from unexpected sources and places. I mention vulnerability not to be cynical, but to be accurate. In spite of the anger of the political world and today's zeitgeist, most people are still well intentioned and delighted to help when they perceive a sincere need.

Fourth, use online networking to increase the transparency of what you do. Most people are fascinated to learn how something works behind the scenes, whether it's cooking or manufacturing or rocket science. You need to think carefully about how you go about this effort, and you need to get the balance right between too little and too much information. But if you can get it right, then you will become a rock star online before you know it.

Fifth, use online networking for humor. Humor is its own justification and is usually received with outsized enthusiasm and returns. I remember a decade ago a lawyer who based a speaking career on knowing more lawyer jokes than anyone else. The last I heard, he had assembled something like five hundred of them. He understood that his audiences would be thinking along those lines anyway, so he beat them to the funny bone and outdid them—and succeeded beyond anyone's expectation.

Of course, there must always be caveats. To do this sort of online networking well, you need to follow a few basic rules of tact and decorum. These become particularly important in the slippery, fast-changing world of social media.

Be consistent. Remember, trust is fragile online. The merest sign of inconsistency can turn an audience off. Don't make the mistake of thinking that being human online means being as human as people can be face-to-face.

Observe propriety. Here, it helps to be just a touch holier than the rest. Don't curse, don't use off-color humor, and so on, unless those practices are well accepted in your world. And it's surprising how people who don't mind the occasional curse in a small group will suddenly become excessively dainty and proper in a public setting, especially when a professional situation is involved. Don't take the chance.

Don't overstay your welcome. One of the great risks of especially successful social networkers is that they become relentless and never-ending. What is charming in the right proportions can become instantly tedious when it's too much. Decide what an appropriate flow of social media networking is for your world, and stick to it.

Successful online relationships begin face-to-face. This idea is hard to accept in the online world, but the best way to establish online relationships is to begin in the real world. If you've got a team that is going to be working on a vital project for a year and a half, and it's distributed all over the world, from Singapore to France to California, then bite the financial bullet and bring everyone together face-to-face. This simple (and potentially expensive) technique can save enormous amounts of money and time down the project road, in efficiency and cooperation.

But don't just meet; you need to do a couple of things to establish trust and connection, and these tasks work much better face-to-face. So pack them into your first meeting if you can. If not, get them done as quickly as you can in subsequent online meetings.

Begin with the big picture. As Simon Sinek brilliantly established in his book *Start with Why*, people need to understand what they're working toward.[5] It's that simple. Tell them why they're there—or better yet, get them to figure it out—and you're well on the way to creating a team.

Give people personal connections. You can accomplish this essential step in creating a successful online team by sending around a questionnaire and getting everyone to talk about hobbies, interests, and personal circumstances outside work. We're more likely to bond with people we have multiple connections with. Do we like similar kinds of music? Do we share the same taste in movies? What kind of sports do we root for? These topics don't need to be complicated, and most people are happy to offer up this sort of information, consistent with their cultural mores and communication patterns.

Set the working ground rules. It's absolutely vital that online teams spend a real amount of time talking about the rules, expectations, rewards, and punishments for working together. Peer pressure happens automatically in teams when they're face-to-face, but it doesn't get established online, because the peer question itself is too vexed in a virtual setting. It's hard to tell what the hierarchy is, who is naturally likely to take charge, and who will cheerfully be a worker bee. You need to sort those questions out deliberately and with great tact for an online team to function well.

Create a safe place to talk. The weakest form of trust gets created when everyone comes individually to the boss to vent. It's much better (and much more work) to encourage people to vent together, because of the trust this shared practice creates. You need a virtual safe place to establish a team that can deal effectively with the inevitable issues that will come up, especially under the pressure of recalcitrant problems. Set that safe place up as somewhere deliberately marked off from the rest of your communications. Consider whether to make it anonymous; there are risks and rewards both ways.

Mark milestones, successes, and celebrations. Just as larger cultures have holidays and other celebrations, you need to create a more modest version of New Year's, monthly milestones, celebrations of successes, and so on. It's far, far better to err on the side of excessive praise and reward than it is to leave achievement unnoticed and unacknowledged.

Share other kinds of time together besides work. Food is a particularly important human sharing mechanism to build trust. It's no accident that most important negotiations on the world stage begin with a meal together. Numerous cultures have deep emotional and even religious associations with food. If you haven't shared meals together, it is highly unlikely that you can have a multidimensional relationship of trust and commitment. But don't stop at food. Use cultural differences as a fun way to learn about each other's cultures, share time together, and establish deeper bonds. Begin, for example, by circulating a brief set of questions on favorite holidays, top holiday destinations in each country, and cultural hot spots.

Let everyone lead, train, and be the expert for the rest of the team. Part of creating trust is the essential emotional connection of responsibility. If I've trained you in some aspect of our work life, I will feel more responsible for your success. It's a way of strengthening personal investment in the team. Don't spend all your time running the show. Share the spotlight, get everyone involved, and watch the connections become stronger and stronger.

As the leader, you must set the standard. Of course, the leader of the team will be looked to for behavior signals online as well as in person. The signals are harder to pick up online, but the team members will nonetheless attempt to learn as much about the leader as possible to understand what's expected of them. You need to set the standard for personal honesty, candor, confidence, trust, and the other positive attributes you want to inculcate throughout the project. Begin with a story that reveals something about you. Be honest and instant about your mistakes. Own everything.

Make allowances for language and culture differences. You need to get in the habit of overcompensating in this area, especially if the organization is dominated by one country's employees. "Of course, we Americans are always way too positive, but I do think this is the best team ever created by MegaCorp and we're going to set a new standard. But before I get carried away, let's hear from a more pessimistic group. Some might say more honest. Will the French weigh in now, please?" The touch has to be light and just right, but if you can surface these intercultural issues immediately and repeatedly, you will save endless amounts of silent sabotage later on.

Make allowances for differing work schedules, inputs, and communication styles. The online channel magnifies rather than minimizes the need for recognition of all the sorts of human differences time, space, and culture can create. It is far better to err on the side of overcompensation for any potential differences than it is to do less.

There is much work to be done at the beginning of a team project—or any kind of online relationship. It's much more efficient and productive to get these difficult background issues taken care of face-to-face. But if you must cover them online, then create checklists of all the possible ways in which cultural differences might impede your progress, and talk them through with the team. Skill levels, working schedules, time differences, candor levels, trust levels, communication styles, work demands, speed of decision making, leadership styles, gender issues—the list goes on and on. Deal with them openly and completely, or let them destroy the team from within later on.

The ultimate goal with all this trust-establishing and team-building work (or only trust-establishing work, in the case of a client or customer relationship) is to get people to commit to one another. Once we've done the work to get the trust engine revved up and running, what else can we do to solidify relationships online? And how can we get customers and clients to sign on at a similar, early point in the relationship, when trust seems to be developing but we need an extra push to get the commitment? With thanks to Robert Cialdini and his wonderful classic, *Influence: The Psychology of Persuasion*, here are some ways to close the deal from the real world that still work well online.[6]

Use social validation. People look to others to see what they should do, both in the real world and virtually. Online ratings and reviews are a powerful way to influence behavior. Making clear what the team values are—or what other clients and customers are doing, in a sales situation—will help push people toward commitment.

Always remember the golden rule of reciprocity. If somebody gives you something, it's highly likely that you will feel obliged to give something in return. This strong feeling of cooperation allows people to connect, commit, and support each other. Giving a gift increases the likelihood that others will reciprocate by giving you something. This is a deep truth of human experience, wherever humans are to be found.

Tease and build interest with scarcity. If there is limited availability of something, we assume it is more valuable and we want it even more. We see this scarcity invoked all the time on e-commerce sites. "Last one in stock" and "limited time only" are familiar phrases. Restricting information to members only or charging a fee are other ways to add value to your content. If something is inaccessible or forbidden, then we really want it! The allure of scarcity bears out online and in the real world, both for teams and for clients.

But always be consistent—first, last, and foremost. Use consistency to gain trust and commitment. Because people like to think they are consistent in their actions, if you ask someone to commit to something small first, then it will be easier to get a larger commitment from the individual later. The benefits of consistency apply everywhere.

Try to match your target audience. One of the ways we make decisions is from a position of similarity. You are more likely to listen to and buy from someone who is like you and someone you find attractive. Similarity builds rapport. If we feel people are similar to us in background or values, we tend to like them more. To persuade people, the stories and photos on a website need to match the target audience or reflect who the audience wants to be. This kind of human connection is far easier to establish in person because it happens automatically. We size up the other person and decide, "Yes, this person is like me" or "No, this person is not like me." Online, you have to work harder to find points of similarity.

Use fear of loss to precipitate decision making. When we are emotionally aroused, whether negatively or positively, we are more likely to encode that experience into our long-term memory. Fear of losing motivates us more than does an opportunity to win. The power of fear of loss holds everywhere, but first you have to get people to care about the outcome.

Always tell stories. The best way to get and hold someone's attention is to tell a story. A good story communicates information thoroughly and commits the information to memory. And that's true both in person and online.

Why are we always asking why?

Winning people's trust to get a commitment is an extremely sensitive activity; we humans are always asking why. We care about intent; trust for us is all about knowing what *their*—the other person's or group's—intentions are. Understanding this psychological truth is what Susan Fiske, professor of psychology and public affairs at Princeton University, sees as crucial to fully grasping the trust conundrum: "If you do one untrustworthy thing, it can take a long time to gain people's trust back."[7]

Fiske's research examines two basic dimensions of perception—sociality and morality—both of which affect trust and both of which operate quite differently. Let's take friendliness as an example. There are two explanations for why you're being nice toward me. One is because you are in fact nice, and the second is because it's the social and desirable thing to do; you want something from me.

When it comes to trustworthiness, people are generally deemed to be trustworthy; it's the default in our human psychology to trust one another. And while there are cultural variations in trust (Americans are faster and more likely to trust than are people from other cultures) and the circle of trust may vary, trustworthiness still remains the default. Problems occur, however, when someone deviates from that default. If you show yourself to be deceptive and untrustworthy, there's no quick cure; these qualities become part of who you are, thus making you socially undesirable.

As Fiske explains, "you can be an absent-minded genius, as long as you do something really smart once in a while. However, an untrustworthy person can't do something trustworthy and then automatically be known as trustworthy."

Fundamentally, it takes a long time to win people's trust back after a failure or betrayal, and you have to behave with complete trustworthiness at some self-sacrifice before people can trust you again. This is true for individuals as well as for companies.

Don't confuse the short term and the long term

In the short term, companies will experience ups and downs requiring them to demonstrate to their customer or client base that they're willing to take a short-term loss to have a long-term relationship with the customer or client. The companies that have gotten into trouble publicly are those that hide things because in the short term it's easier to hide. But in the long term, they come to seem untrustworthy as a result—the very definition of short-sighted behavior. Remember, we humans care most about our reading of your worthy intentions—or the opposite. We want to know if you are interested not only in your own outcome, but also at least somewhat in the larger public good.

There can arise a virtual feedback loop if companies take on an issue that affects them. A ski manufacturer might champion doing something about climate change so that the snow will continue to fall on ski slopes, for example. The feedback loop is even stronger if companies support issues that are seen as wider social goods at the time. That same ski company might speak out in favor of diversity or gender equality, for example.

So how does this aspect of trust change in the virtual world? If the automatic default is still to be trusted, does this work between two people communicating virtually? Fiske says it does:

> I don't think it differs so much, but I think trustworthiness in general is harder to establish virtually than it is in person. This is due to the fact that trustworthiness has these two components to them. Sociality is easier to establish in person as you make eye contact and smile politely and so forth. Whereas online, it's a more stripped-down version of interaction. You see a webpage that looks friendly, but where are its worthy intentions? To make it trustworthy, you need feedback, to be responsive and have 24-7 people on call. These are all examples of showing worthy intentions. It demonstrates that brands, companies, and people are there not only to sell you things, but to respond to you as well. Ultimately, this is being trustworthy.[8]

The opposite of trust—betrayal—works much the same way. In the virtual world, sadly, people betray each other in a similar fashion. "When you meet in person, establishing worthy intentions is down to the fact that you trek up to some place, have dinner, and spend some time together," Fiske says. "If you say that you're going to skip dinner and work, that's not very friendly, nor if you spend your whole time in a meeting answering your email. And while this is easy to do when communicating over the phone or Skype, there are telltale signs when it happens. People often answer their email on a conference call, which you can tell because there's a lag when you address them." Your worthy intentions are now shattered, and as a brand, a company, or an individual, you have deviated from the trustworthy perception. And these little betrayals quickly add up to a complete lack of trust in the virtual world—indeed, much more quickly than they might in person.

Only use humor that works across cultures and online

Is humor an effective way to build connection, trust, and commitment? And how well does it translate across cultures, ages, ethnic groups, and all the other ways humans divide themselves up? A laugh is always good, unless it is wrung reluctantly out of your listener because it's cheap or tacky or insults a cultural norm. Avoid the worst mistakes of traditional one-liners and cheap irony, replacing them instead with witty humor that works and wins audiences over to your side.

Traditional jokes with punch lines are the hardest to pull off. They offer the greatest risks of giving offense or simply failing because the timing—or the cultural understanding—is off. So, avoid them unless you know exactly what you're doing and whom you're talking to. Instead, consider irony. At its worst, irony is a cheap, easy way to get a chuckle and avoid making a commitment. At its best, irony is a memorable way for the alienated to comment on the in crowd, the powerless to bring down the powerful, and the hip to skewer the not-so-hip.

There are three rules for making irony memorable rather than cheap.

Create an overarching story that is different from what you're apparently talking about. This narrative misdirection enables you to take an ironic (because it's distant) stance toward your real topic.

Something important has to be at stake. But what's at stake can be anything important that the speaker-narrator cares about. Cheap irony has nothing behind it—no alternative that it is proposing. Powerful irony points to a better way.

The viewpoint has to run counter to the one held by those currently in power. When the viewpoint stands in contrast to the popular one, the irony has more impact. Irony can give a surprisingly strong voice to those who are less powerful, less engaged, or less popular.

But the best humor both in person and online derives from the moment itself. By definition, then, you have to be ready in the moment, and thus any advice offered here will be too little, too late. Nonetheless, I have three suggestions for finding the right witty comment in that moment.

Don't try too hard. Wit flows from passion for the subject. If you feel strongly about something, you will find wit in the subject and you will share it with your audience.

Wit is all about upending expectations. The wit is in the surprise.

To be witty, take the subject, but not yourself, seriously. Nothing kills humor faster than someone's taking himself or herself too seriously. A small dose of self-deprecation, or a clear indication that you care more about the issue at hand than you do about accolades for yourself, helps people trust you.

Come to think of it, those are great suggestions for making online relationships work, as well.

Practical fixes

The update video

The ideal way to establish trust is to mix the real and virtual worlds. But it's not always possible to begin an essentially virtual relationship with in-person trust building. Budgets and time limitations constrain many organizations, making it difficult to get the ideal combination.

Instead, you can create brief (thirty- to sixty-second) videos that show you doing something in your real locale, connecting with local food, culture, sights, or situations in a way that anchors you in your environment. Your whole team should do the same and share these videos regularly. This virtual library of real moments will help everyone on your team learn to trust and connect with one another—the steps to commitment.

Use your mobile phone to create the video. Keep it very short, and keep it light. Share an authentic moment, not a slickly produced commercial.

The cultural questionnaire

This set of questions is not meant to be an exhaustive test of differences among cultures. It is intended simply to make the process of exploring cultural differences easier. You might circulate these questions before an initial meeting of a cross-cultural team, for example, or make them the focus of the first meeting itself. The idea is to start conversations, not administer an exam.

1. What are the three most important historical stories about your country or culture?

2. Which languages are spoken?

3. What are a few of your most important cultural dos and don'ts?

4. Does your country or culture love or hate to negotiate? How does that work?

5. Do you appreciate formality or informality? What are the appropriate forms of address?

6. Who is equal and who is not in your culture or country?

7. Tell me about punctuality: Is your culture always, sometimes, or never on time?

8. How does your government work?

9. Is gift giving common or uncommon in your country or culture?

10. How long does it take someone to decide to act or not act in your country or culture?

11. How do you greet a family member, a close friend, a business acquaintance?

12. What are the appropriate norms of dress for business, for relaxing, for socializing?

13. What is your country's favorite sport?

14. Is it acceptable to wager on that sport?

15. How do people spend their days off in your country or culture?

16. What's your favorite music?

17. Who is your favorite writer?

18. What's your favorite movie?

19. Who is one of your heroes?

20. How does your country or culture express emotions?

CHAPTER SUMMARY

- Driving to commitment is more difficult online than in person.

- The news is not all bad; surprisingly, perhaps, social media helps cement business relationships, and people with a stronger social media presence tend to be more successful.

- To use social media successfully online for business, play by the rules, be authentic, don't take yourself too seriously, and know when to quit.

- You can drive commitment online using well-established rules of social influence just as you do in person.

- We basically treat companies as if they were people; we form emotional bonds with them and feel betrayed if they break our trust.

- Trust comes after connection and credibility, and before commitment.

- Use humor strategically to strengthen connections.

PART TWO

SPECIFIC TECHNIQUES
FOR SPECIFIC
DIGITAL CHANNELS

EMAIL, EMAIL ALTERNATIVES, AND TEXTING

When email first worked its way into most workplaces, it was part of a dedicated system, a set of interconnected computers limited to little more than email itself, with batch runs of data at night and the infamous sprocket paper—like a slightly more flexible telex machine. Then desktop computers became the norm, and finally laptops and smartphones.

Along the way, our relationship with email was gradually transformed. What began as an effort to make communication of written stuff—scientific papers, hard ideas, things that needed to be precisely expressed—easier between scientists became a way for the rest of us to communicate everything in and around the world of work, family, and social relationships.

That's when the problems began. Soon there was too much of it, all that communication, and at the same time it frequently misfired. We all suffer from information overload. And occasionally, we suffer from its opposite—information deprivation. Waiting for the email that never comes, we experience a peculiarly modern form of the disease that is as old as Adam and Eve—starving for something in the midst of plenty.

We've all had our feelings hurt by some email communication, and we probably have hurt other people's feelings. We've revealed in emails some secrets that we shouldn't have shared, and we've been told secrets that we shouldn't have heard.

Email communication, in short, is simultaneously messy, imperfect, overwhelming, and impoverished. It's too much and too little at the same time. It was begun for a different purpose, was hijacked to fulfill a need for more and faster communication, and became a blunt instrument that no one can do without.

Now, of course, there are many additional, similar instruments—texting, Slack, and various other attempts to improve on email, but their basic purport is to replace immediate, face-to-face communication with a text-based, virtual, asynchronous alternative.

We'll talk about Slack later in this chapter, but overall, how well does text-based communication work? The answer is, unsurprisingly, not very well at all. The problems are inherent in the nature of the communication medium. So what can you do to anticipate, restore, and otherwise employ email so that it actually works, if not precisely as intended, because it's too late for that, then at least not in a mutually self-destructive manner?

First, know what you're trying to achieve. Don't use email or other text-based communication media just because they're the cheapest, easiest, most convenient form of media around. Instead, spend a few moments or, in the case of a team, a few meetings figuring out what you're trying to do and, accordingly, what form of communication will work best.

Tweeting, for example, has the advantage of immediacy and the overwhelming disadvantage of inadequacy for virtually everything beyond one of those irritating business slogans that are the stuff of everyday chatter on social media. *Do more with less. Leaders eat last. Always tell the truth so you don't have to remember what you've said.* Don't use tweets for communicating anything that requires any subtlety at all. Period. Even though Twitter expanded the permitted size of a tweet beyond the original 140 characters, tweets are too ephemeral to be trusted with substantive content.

Email can function usefully as part of a communication quiver for a business team that's separated by geography, but it shouldn't be the only form. Never use email for emotionally important tasks like beginning relationships or repairing or terminating them.

Second, never email a brick at the last minute. One of the most irritating features of modern digital life is the last-minute communication. It goes like this. You're heading to a meeting at 9:00 a.m. Perhaps you're in traffic, and surreptitiously scanning email in the slowest moments. (*Don't! Put that phone down! You're a hazard to yourself and others!*) At 8:15, you receive the following email:

> I'm not sure you'll have a chance to look at this, but in case you do, here's a report that could entirely 180 our approach to the client at 9:00 this morning. It's long at 27 pages, but there's a 3-page summary at the beginning that will give you the gist of it. See you at 9:00 sharp!

The implicit rudeness of this communication—*I don't care enough about you or these matters to give you time to absorb them properly because your opinion doesn't really matter to me*—should make it a no-no for everyone, but we don't always meet the high standards we set for ourselves, do we? Don't send last-minute reading bricks to others, and don't read them if they come from someone else. That's a rule we all need to live by.

Third, don't send hot emails. We are all familiar with the perils of the email sent too quickly, hitting the "reply all" button when we meant to reserve that snarky comment for the author of the original email, not the entire team. Or we've responded in haste and anger to something and regretted it later.

The solution to this problem is pretty simple in theory and tough in practice: self-restraint. Introduce a policy of waiting until you've cooled off. Or writing an email and sending it the next day, after you've slept on it and had a chance to reread it. To be able to do that, of course, you need to build back in some of the time that our friction-free universe has allowed us to cut out.

The time pressure will never go away, but for any kind of virtual communication (email, text, voice mail, video messages, etc.), the more you can build in a waiting period, the less likely you are to send a communication that embarrasses you, ends a relationship, or terminates a career.

Fourth, establish a virtual message hierarchy. Try to use a channel that's appropriate for a particular message when you need to convey something. Use a text message to say "running 10 minutes late." Use an email to say "Attached is the first draft of the report for your consideration." Use an audioconference to update the team in brief weekly sessions, complete with emotional channels deliberately built back in. Use a video session for deeper discussions, rehearsals, and other more substantial interactions. Finally, if you must communicate delicate, emotional, or otherwise fraught matters via virtual channels, create an additional virtual space for the inclusion and consideration of emotions.

Fifth, consider the use of emoji. These visual tools are a crude first attempt for people to put back into text messaging and social media the emotions that too often get misinterpreted or left out. Make sure you include a section of your communication where, at the minimum, emotions can be exchanged, with emoji or in some other way. Make it an emotionally safe space if at all possible. And make it a requirement. The sender needs to indicate how he or she meant the communication to be seen emotionally, both in what emotional state it was sent and in how it's meant to be received. And the receiver needs a space to show how the message was indeed received.

It may seem clunky at first to force yourself to do this extra emotional work, but when you think about the time, money, and human desperation involved in sending, receiving, and untangling unintentionally hurtful messages, for example, the work is clearly work worth doing. You have to deliberately, and imperfectly, put the body-language channel back in where the virtual world has removed it.

Of course, email relies on good writing. What are the rules of good writing that particularly apply to email? Let's look at some of them now.

Maintain clarity, a viewpoint, a clear idea, hierarchical thinking, and grace of expression

Written communications should be kept short when possible. Good communication is an exchange of attention for insight. You email on the fly while you're doing something else; when you're in a hurry; when you're trying to deal with many issues at once; and when you're exhausted from computers, iPads, phones, and other devices. You compose emails in the airport, in the car when you shouldn't, or anyplace else where you can snatch some time. The list of impediments to thoughtful, elegant, concise prose is as long as everything you have to do. You can't pay enough attention to the job of creating the email, and your recipient can't pay enough attention to the job of reading it.

Clarity is the cornerstone of good writing

Good email communication begins with clarity—like all communications. To achieve clarity in an email communication, you must first have a clear thought. Alternatively, you can write to find out what you're thinking. If you follow the latter course, then you owe it to yourself and your readers to always be prepared to edit, to rewrite what you have written.

Don't say, "The final success of the outcome will be ascertained by a careful consideration of a combination of all the inputs, the experiences of the participants along the way, and the specific parameters of the analysis of all the measurable takeaways, deltas, and observable changes in the gathered data relevant to the experiment."

Do say, "The results will determine the success of the experiment."

Clarity and brevity necessarily go together. The more you write, the greater the chances that you will write something hard to understand or that someone will misunderstand. It's a commonplace that the pace of life and work just keeps on increasing. This observation means that we often lose track of the big picture or that we simply don't know what we don't know. These challenges hugely increase the need for someone to keep us straight—to give us a few simple rules to keep our heads in the game, above water, and screwed on tight. And oh yes—get it done in twenty reading minutes, please, like the written equivalent of a TED talk.

When you're done with your first pass at a written communication, put it aside for at least sixty seconds. Then go back and reread it, edit it, and make sure it is clear. Look particularly for emotional clarity. Remember, it is the emotions that are too often lacking in our virtual life, and they are hard to get right in an email. Put an extra sentence in deliberately at the end to make your emotions clear if you fear they may not be: "I mean this sincerely; I'm not being sarcastic."

A final caveat on clarity: lots of research suggests that people often misunderstand each other in email or overestimate the success of an email communication. For example, recent research shows that people believe email requests are just as effective as face-to-face—but the reverse is true.[1] So even as you use the medium, keep in mind that it is not as effective as speaking to the person live. Email is just more efficient. Another recent study showed that in-person conversations or phone calls made the person sound smarter than the same script conveyed over email.[2]

Indeed, overall, one in three workers has misjudged the tone of an email.[3] Many of these people got upset about what they thought was a colleague insulting them or saying something personal—when nothing personal was intended at all.

Research has further shown that ambiguous emails increase stress in the workplace and lead to more friction between coworkers.[4] When you're constantly wondering whether your colleagues are upset, or if you're interpreting their comments as sarcastic or rude, of course you're going to feel stressed-out.

Why is it so difficult to correctly judge the tone or subtext of an email? We tend to overestimate both our ability to convey the tone we want to convey in an email and our ability to judge other people's tones.[5] We think we know exactly what we're saying, and we think we know what other people are trying to say—but we're wrong. Why? The answer is egocentrism. Researchers Justin Kruger of New York University, Nicholas Epley of the University of Chicago, and their colleagues have studied the issue and found that we are helplessly stuck in our own perspectives.[6]

Kruger and Epley had people email statements, either sarcastic or serious, to a partner. The senders thought their messages would come through clearly 78 percent of the time. But they were wrong. Their partners understood the writers' intended tone only 56 percent of the time. The partners might just as well have flipped a coin. And even worse, the people reading these emails thought *they* had gotten the tone right 90 percent of the time.

We think we know what our colleagues (and our friends and maybe even our partners) are trying to say in emails and text messages, but we're wrong. We think our own communications are crystal clear, but we're also wrong. What can we do about this communication gap? One simple answer is to get on the phone. But, of course, we all need to send emails; it's a fact of modern life. Kruger and Epley found one possible solution: try reading your emails out loud a few times, in different tones, including offended, sarcastic, or angry tones, before you send them. The researchers found that reading a message in a way you didn't intend makes it easier for you to step outside your own perspective and appreciate that you might be misinterpreted. And that's a first step toward better communication.

Make sure your writing has a point of view

What we humans care about fundamentally is each other's intent. When you write, figure out your point of view, and make it clear. State your point at the top, if possible. If not, present it as soon as possible. The alternative looks and feels to the receivers like sandbagging, and they feel betrayed. Don't do it.

Don't say, "Thanks for coming to the meeting yesterday. Your participation was helpful, and I think all the participants got something out of the entire meeting and the focus on the deliverables and structure for the reorg going forward. But next time, don't show up late."

Do say, "I was upset that you were late, but the meeting was productive, and everyone was satisfied with the outcome of the reorg."

To make sure you do have a clear point of view, you need to find moments of passion. One of the best ways to keep your writing interesting is not to think about your passion in general—everyone knows you need passion—but rather to provide contrasting moments of calm and passion throughout the email. Contrast is memorable; a harangue all begins to sound the same after a while. Give people variety by working yourself up to a fine sizzle at key moments—but not all the time.

Tell the recipients something they don't know—but don't tell them everything you know. We all love to learn a little insider knowledge or a factoid that adds a bit of depth and complexity to a well-known story. The radio personality Paul Harvey made a whole career out of telling "the rest of the story," adding little-known facts to familiar tales of historical personages and famous people. ("The name of that awkward lawyer who failed in business so many times? Abraham Lincoln.")[7]

But we only crave a *little* extra knowledge. Too many writers dump way too much information on the reader. Restraint is key. Again, keep it as short as possible—but no shorter.

Build suspense by starting a story or promising an insight and then delivering it later. This technique works for Dan Brown, and it will work for you. Introduce something—"In the next paragraph, I'll show you how to double your net worth in six months with a simple trick"—and then follow through on the promise. Don't overuse this technique, and don't commit the cardinal sin of upselling—promising "six ways to increase your

IQ if you buy this other course I'm selling" —because upselling abuses the relationship between speaker and audience.

Finally, keep it real. Authenticity begins with clarity about your own values, goals, and needs. In this era, we demand more of one another—more authenticity, more emotion, and, yes, even more self-disclosure. You get to choose what you reveal. And we don't want too much, but we need to know that you're real. We need a point of view.

Make sure you have a clear idea

I always recommend beginning to work on a text-based communication with a single sentence. What's the point you want to make? If you don't know what that is, then you're not ready to write. We're impatient, so we jump into writing too quickly just to keep up with our email and to tick things off the to-do list.

Once you know what the point is, jot it down in a sentence. You're now ready to write, even if you never actually use that sentence in the document. For political reasons, you might not want to state your point right away, preferring to begin with mutually agreed-upon ideas, but you will have to get to it eventually.

But don't hold off too long. We demand greater and greater transparency from our leaders and even from our email correspondents. We don't like to feel manipulated. This demand has huge implications not only for internal communications, but also for external emails to clients and other business connections, who want to work more openly than ever before.

Part of your point should always be to make your intent clear and to show that it is both consistent and empathetic to the reader.

Don't say, "We've been working on all aspects of the project, from the initial idea to the various ways in which it will affect all the employees and the parking structure. There's a whole set of imponderables that will need to be considered down the line before we go to the planning commission and the public. We will require an additional set of planning sessions as well as lengthening the timeline to include extra public assessment time as well as the sheer scope of things, which has increased."

Do say, "Building the parking garage is going to take longer than we thought because it has turned out to be more controversial than we thought."

Do the hierarchical thinking for your audience

What is hierarchical thinking? It's showing what's more important and what's less important. It's distinguishing between the main point and the detail. It means that if you tell your readers that something is important, you also should tell them what they don't have to know.

Hierarchical thinking keeps track of where you are. One of the kindest things you can do as a writer for your readers is to let them know where you are in the text. Number your points. Tell your readers what they are in for. Make your progress clear. Tell them you're halfway through, as in "Let me pause here for a moment at the halfway mark to recap briefly."

A recent study showed that memory is a zero-sum game.[8] We forget one old thing for every new thing we learn. That's distressing, perhaps, for writers—most of us—because, essentially, we're asking our readers to forget things as fast as we pour new ideas into their heads.

But before we writers throw in the text towel and stop trying to get our readers to remember anything at all, it's worth turning this science on its head. Rather than seeing this zero-sum quality as a discouraging fact, in the right light, we can find it very good news indeed.

How so? Modern businesspeople trying desperately to absorb all the information that comes their way every day are pictures of distraction. Knowing what's essential to remember for modern life and success is a much harder puzzle than the acts of remembering and forgetting themselves.

Understood in this context, forgetting as much as you remember is a mercy and a necessity for survival in our information-rich modern world. More than that, *helping people forget the right things* becomes an important job in a world like the one we inhabit now.

Writers, take heart. By putting new ideas into the heads of your correspondents (and thus forcing them to forget old ideas), you're helping clean the cerebral house, a highly important task given the speed and volume of new ideas.

Don't say, "To understand the reasons for the upset around the parking garage project, we have to understand that the public was kept in the dark for too long about the purpose of the building. They were expecting an award-winning art museum, and instead they got a giant parking structure. This switch felt like a lie to the public, and so people were understandably upset. This anger, and the increased tax burden already felt as a result of the increases over the last year, anyway, contributed to the problem. Also, the mayor's lack of support for the project was crippling after her initial apparent support."

Do say, "There are three reasons for the public controversy over the parking structure. First, and most important, the public was misled about the real nature of the building. Second, the mayor at first offered and then withdrew her support. And third, taxes have been rising recently, so any spending is an issue."

Offer your readers grace of expression

Grace of expression comes from practice, editing, clarity, brevity, and a few basic values—authenticity, consistency, transparency, empathy, and connection—that are especially important in the virtual world.

Authenticity. Grace of expression begins with authenticity—personal clarity about what is important to you. Despite today's demands to share more of ourselves, you can choose what to reveal. There is a balance between sharing too much and not enough. But people want to know that you're real. You must be authentic.

Consistency. Today, in our rush to get things done, we use mental shortcuts for things that we used to do much more slowly. For example, we tend to use consistency as an imperfect test for establishing trust, a quality that is ever more important to us in a low-trust world. We accept that we ourselves can change our minds and suffer bad moods, but we're much less likely to accept this kind of natural inconsistency from others. No waffling.

Transparency. We demand greater and greater transparency from our colleagues, leaders, partners, and other associates. This demand has huge implications not only for internal documents but also for external missives to customers, external stakeholders, and the public. We must be prepared to write it like it is and find grace in that expression of openness.

Empathy. All of us are expected to show greater understanding of, and greater sensitivity to, more and more perspectives than ever before. Being caught out with a lack of empathy for someone or some group can completely derail a text—and a career.

Connection. Our readers expect more than just a text from us. When they follow up with questions, they expect a quick response, any time, day or night, weekdays or weekends. People expect to be able to connect with everyone today. All the time.

Internalize these rules gracefully, and you'll go a long way toward becoming the true voice of your era.

Don't say, "All employees using the company kitchen are responsible for taking care of the whole space, which means being considerate of all the other users, taking care of your own stuff, such as making sure that you throw out any expired food or leftovers that have been in the fridge more than a couple of days. It also means wiping down the counters, putting any and all dishes in the dishwasher, rinsing out coffee cups to control the waste and smell of old coffee grounds that employees have complained about, and removing and adequately sorting the recyclables from the nonrecyclable waste."

Do say, "Let's all work together to keep the kitchen spotless."

A few basic rules can prevent email backfires

A few final rules for successful text-based communications.

Avoid sending out mass mailings. Too many of us get cc'ed and bcc'ed on endless all-team, all-unit, and all-company emails that someone was doing the CYA thing on and that we really don't have to read. If something is important, send it as an individual message to each recipient.

Don't say anything via email that you would be horrified to see online in a public forum. Email is not secure, as any number of executives in Hollywood, in the business world, and in politics can tell you, to their enormous chagrin.

An email or text is not the best format for a vigorous discussion. If you want that, set up a meeting or a phone call.

If you want a response to your email, make this point clear, and don't send it to lots of recipients. If you want several people to comment on a document, say, then put it in a shared discussion folder with format control to avoid the nightmare of multiple versions.

Don't rant in emails, and don't respond angrily to rants. Take a deep breath, and go see the person to talk it over if you know who the person is. If you don't, then don't respond at all.

Should you be using something else besides email?

The way we communicate in the modern office continues to evolve. Where once we had to walk down the hall or pick up the phone to talk to our colleagues, now we can quickly fire off an email from a desktop, laptop, or mobile device. Email is so easy to send, in fact, that it's become a deluge. Step away from your desk for a moment, and you may get more emails than you can possibly respond to. As a result, many offices now also use chat programs like Google Hangouts (formerly Gchat) and Slack.

Why Slack is so popular

Slack started life as an internal collaboration tool for a team that was working on developing an online game. Its name derives from an acronym: searchable log of all conversation and knowledge.[9] As the phrase implies, Slack is a team chat program that's searchable, and it allows users to upload and share images, files, and snippets of code. You can tag a coworker to make sure the person sees an important comment. You can create specific channels for teams and subteams and can direct-message a specific user. Created for developers, the program is still particularly popular with them, but it has spread to many tech-savvy offices.

One of those offices is Klick Health, a health marketing agency.[10] The company of roughly seven hundred people uses Gmail-based email, Google Hangouts, and Slack. Employees say that Slack spread organically. "Slack did not come top down," says Keith Liu, Klick's senior vice president for products and innovation. The company does have an internal chat platform, but chats posted there are visible to the entire company, so the internal app is not used as much for day-to-day communication. "I treat it [the proprietary platform] very much like companywide email," Liu says. It's like replying all to seven hundred people, he says.

Because Slack is an outside app, employees say that it feels more private even than Google Hangouts or email. Employees can install the Slack app on their phones without installing a device administrator (and giving their employer some control over their device) the way they would have to install something to use their corporate email on a personal device. Technically, managers have access to employees' corporate email accounts, but not their Slack accounts. These privacy features help contribute to a sense that Slack is more casual and less formal than email.

Most people also tend to get fewer notifications from Slack than they do from email, so it feels less burdensome. "The main benefit is the signal-to-noise ratio," says Yan Fossat, Klick's vice president of labs. "This morning, I had six thousand unread emails," Fossat says. People know he's more likely to see a Slack message because the volume is more manageable, he says.

Of course, this lower volume does create an expectation that every Slack message will be read. The deluge of email can serve as a convenient excuse for missing or failing to respond to a message, but a similar excuse doesn't seem to work for Slack, Klick employees say. "The problem with that is, it's a timeline," Liu says. If you step away from a group chat for a while, you may have to scroll back quite a way to catch up on everything. And if you don't, you're going to miss things. In a contentious situation, Slack can almost be "weaponized," Liu says. "There's no defense against" a colleague pointing out that the information was posted on Slack a week ago, Liu says. Even if you didn't see the comment, the implication is that you should have.

The expectation that everyone will stay up-to-date on a chat program like Slack may come in part from the fact that the app is, or can be, a real-time communication platform. Slack and other chat programs feel more immediate or urgent than email does, Klick employees say. It feels acceptable to wait a week to respond to an email, Fossat says, but a chat seems to demand an immediate response. For Fossat, Slack is somewhere between an email and a Google Hangouts session. He says he would respond to a text message or Google Hangouts message right away, a Slack message within a couple of hours, and an email within twenty-four hours or so.

Slack and other chat programs seem to allow for richer communication than what email provides, Klick employees say. "Nobody would describe email as a messaging platform or as a collaboration tool," Liu says. "Slack is a collaboration tool." That's one reason developers tend to like it so much. The chat app allows colleagues to share the files or code they're working on, or share the ticket for a task, and continue to chat about how to approach the problem at hand. This capability helps make space for more problem solving than is possible in a medium like email, where only one person can "talk" at a time and where it's easy to talk at cross-purposes if two or more people respond to the same message at the same time with different ideas.

Employees at Klick also say that it's easier to get a sense of tone and personality in a chat program than it is over email. Everyone has that colleague who comes across as abrupt or even rude over email. "On channels like Slack and Gchat, their abruptness can come across, well, it's like a dry humor," Liu says. Something about the real-time immediacy of Slack or its organic spread and less official feel means that people tend to communicate less formally and more conversationally in chat. People are also much more likely to share gifs or memes in chat programs than with email, Klick employees say.

It's also more acceptable to cut to the chase in chat. Perhaps because you're in and out of the program all day, it's socially acceptable to dispense with the small talk, whereas in an email, people still feel obliged to include greetings and niceties like "Hope you're well." The brevity of chat, too, may help avoid miscommunication. "The less you say, the less likely it is that they will misunderstand," Fossat says.

Is chat a better way of handling conflict than email is?

When conflict does arise on a team, the chat medium seems to make the conflict easier to manage. Email comes across as a more formal message. Particularly from a manager, a terse email carries a lot of weight, Liu says. "When I'm professionally angry," he says, "I can be professionally angry on Gchat, and it's conversational. But if I end up writing those same things in an email, that becomes a formal missive as opposed to 'That really irked me.'" In a chat, irritation may feel more like a natural part of the ebb and flow of conversation; in an email, particularly from a manager, irritation may feel more like a formal reprimand.

Klick teams tend to invite their clients into project-specific Slack channels once the teams have established a working relationship with a client. Establishing this type of communication with a client has numerous benefits, Klick employees say. For one thing, it's transparent. Anyone in a Slack channel can see all comments, so "the client feels like you're being more honest with them," Liu says. Using Slack can also create a sense of exclusivity, where you and the client become part of an in group. "It actually is a closer relationship," Liu says. "It allows for more serendipitous and closer communication." Fossat agrees: "You feel closer by being less correct."

Several conclusions emerge from office experiences like Klick's. First of all, the differences between one kind of writing program and another are probably not sufficient to justify the time and expense of switching and training an entire organization in the new software. Second, some kind of texting program to allow people to send out quick queries, comments, shout-outs, and notes to each other is probably essential in today's fast-moving offices. And finally, training your organization to learn not to hit "copy all" every time an email is sent out would be good for business, morale, and efficiency. No one should be receiving six thousand emails a day.

Practical fixes

The "What's in it for me?" move

To increase the impact and memorability of your communications, be they email or any other digital form, you can explicitly inform the audience what's in it for them. Why and how, in short, this piece of information matters to them. Include this information *as a one-sentence headline at the top of the communication.* This technique was discovered by researchers trying to help memory-impaired people remember their daily lives better. In the digital world, we're all a little memory impaired, so this practice of headlining the benefits of the information will help you and your team remember things better. Do it because it will work for you. The researchers called the technique "self-imagining," which sounds a little ominous, but don't let that put you off. It works.

Emoji

As I've encouraged you to do earlier, use emoji. Yes, they run the risk of seeming childish. But they do let the recipient know what you're feeling. And that's incredibly important—way more important than what you're actually saying.

The email cheat sheet

Refer to these guidelines on a regular basis to keep your email writing clear, tight, and effective.

1. Writing needs clarity, a point of view, a point, hierarchical thinking, and grace of expression.

2. Write conversationally, and then revise.

3. Try to make the actor in the sentence the subject of it.

4. Avoid passive constructions for the most part.

5. Take out the fillers and qualifiers.

6. Same with adjectives and adverbs.

7. Start an email, a paragraph, and your sentences with the familiar, the old, the agreed-upon. Then move to the unfamiliar, the new, the debatable.

8. Put the emphasis at the end of sentences and paragraphs when possible.

9. What we humans care about fundamentally is each other's intent. Make your intent clear.

10. Find moments of passion—but don't shout the whole time.

11. Tell the receiver something he or she doesn't know—but don't tell the person everything you know.

12. We only crave a *little* extra knowledge.

13. Build suspense by starting a story or promising an insight and then delivering it later.

14. Keep it real.

15. Begin with a *trigger*, an emotional framing sentence, prompting the reader to want to do something.

16. Then, go into some detail to show that you understand the reader's world.

17. Once the reader is prepared, then hit him or her with the new idea.

18. Then help the reader understand the benefits of the idea.

19. Close a written piece with the action you want to propose.

20. Good writing has authenticity, consistency, transparency, empathy, and connection.

CHAPTER SUMMARY

- Don't automate anything that should contain the personal touch.

- Don't email long communiqués at the last minute.

- Don't send emotionally laden emails or throw other virtual bombs when you're in the heat of passion; wait until you cool down.

- Establish a virtual message hierarchy, and agree with your team on the forms and frequency of your communications.

- Address cultural differences directly; embrace difference.

- Writing is hard; few of us do it well.

- Our modern world requires all of us to become writers.

- Writing needs clarity, a point of view, a clear idea, hierarchical thinking, and grace of expression.

- Write conversationally, and then revise.

- Good writing also has authenticity, consistency, transparency, empathy, and connection.

- There are alternatives to email, but none of them relieve us of the burden of writing.

- Companies that have added software like Slack find that employees have to write and read more, not less.

THE CONFERENCE CALL

In all the lore of online business life, the stories of what your colleagues actually do when they're on conference calls (instead of participating) are legion, lusty, and legend. Put on the mute button, and those virtual people go to real-life town. Partly it's because conference calls are ubiquitous—the low-hanging, rotten fruit of the digital world. And partly it's because they are so boring.

Of course, there are tales of embarrassing rants and even more embarrassing noises. And I read recently of a man who was fired for making an obscene gesture at the phone, not realizing that the video camera was on as he walked in to join the meeting.[1] But my favorite story—and the Golden Ear Award—belongs to the two people that experienced an earthquake while speaking (they were in different places)—and kept going on the call.[2] Probably because everyone was on mute and thus no one was actually there.

Let's look into what needs to happen to the audioconference to make it better.

Just because a technology exists is no reason to embrace it

We begin with a taxonomy. There are, broadly speaking, three kinds of conference calls that merit independent dissection.

First, there's the public conference call. Your chief financial officer (CFO) might run such a call quarterly when he or she is updating the investor community about the company financials. The format on that one is for the CFO and possibly one or two other executives to speak from a prepared text of some sort for ten minutes or longer, followed by an open Q and A session for listeners to ask follow-up questions and kick the financial tires. Because these calls are public, they will be recorded, placed in an archive, saved, and forgotten. But their immediate results can be financially significant for the company or can even make national or international news if the company is routinely in the headlines. The stakes are thus high.

I once worked with a chief executive whose voice was so jarring on the ear that every time he spoke at one of the quarterly conference calls, the stock price would go down a point or two. His voice literally cost the company millions. I'm delighted to tell you that we were able to improve his voice and help the company financials at the same time.

Second, there are conference calls between organizations and their clients or customers, or between various members of a project team that has assembled for a specific period or to accomplish a specific task. It's not a public call, but there are often contractual agreements, sales situations, or other sorts of business issues at stake or being discussed. Here, embarrassing gaffes can have companywide implications if a sale fails because of someone's misbehavior, incompetence, or simple inability to deliver the goods.

The stakes range from high, if a big sale is at stake, to low if the call is more routine.

Third, there are the weekly staff calls. These are the elevator music of the digital work world, commanding little respect and less attention—unless they are run well. The stakes are typically low. Let's talk about how to improve all three types of calls.

Put some life into your voice. It helps many people to have an actual person to talk to in the room with them. You're less likely to drift into a lifeless monotone if you are speaking to someone in person. Having someone in the room with you helps keep the tone conversational and provides variety in your voice, as you naturally do when speaking with someone in person. Standing up helps, too; you're less likely to let your voice drift into a deadly monotone.

Put someone (else) in charge. If you've got people who are designated speakers, don't expect them to also run the conference. Get someone additional to be the MC. The result will be well worth the extra effort involved in having someone to monitor problems, field questions, provide a road map, and so on. An MC should always think of himself or herself as the representative of the audience, asking questions that a reasonable person might wonder about. The MC should also summarize, follow up, coordinate, add in, and generally clean up the conversation as it unfolds. Done well, it's an active role that can transform an audioconference of this ilk into one that is tight, memorable, and well run. The MC might also get into the habit of posting an agenda on a website or some other accessible place for potential participants to peruse ahead of time—and to use as a scorecard along the way during the call.

Put a limit on the formal remarks. Attention spans have apparently shrunk to ten minutes these days.[3] So never go longer than ten minutes with one person's remarks without pausing for questions and comments. And take some questions as you go if there are several speakers. You can come back at the end for a general free-for-all, but do take questions after each speaker, unless you're trying hard to bury something the first speaker is going to say.

For the client call, try having someone from your side act as an advocate for the other side. This person could listen in to pick up on all the unanswered questions, unresolved issues, and unspoken complaints from the other side. If you're the main salesperson, or if you're delivering content, it will be difficult for you to listen with this sort of focus and attention. Leave the job for someone else.

Circulate an agenda in advance, if the MC hasn't, and appoint someone to take notes and send them out to all parties afterward. The agenda will allow participants to pace themselves. The follow-up will give everyone a chance to add and subtract things that are important; it will also provide an important reminder for anything that was agreed on.

Take on or appoint the role of active listener. This is good meeting hygiene in any situation, but it's particularly important on a conference call. An active listener repeats back (usually in a shorter, but not a reductive, way) what he or she has heard and gets confirmation that the impression was accurate.

And there's some personal stuff to get right, too. According to researcher Joshua Feast, CEO of Cogito Corporation, and Sandy Pentland, a Cogito cofounder, what becomes more important when you remove visual cues are two things—prosodic behaviors and the quality of your voice.[4]

Prosodic behaviors are not as terrifying as they sound; they are simply the normal chatting habits that allow us to keep the chat flowing: taking turns, the tempo of the interaction, and, of course, listening. Most of those behaviors are accomplished unconsciously from long habit when we're face-to-face, but when things get virtual, you have to do them intentionally. If you do, all the participants are more likely to feel included, equal partners, and listened to.

The quality of your voice is very important, too. Is your tempo even, do you provide vocal variety, and do you avoid extremes of vocal behavior—shouting, screaming, or hanging up the phone? Pauses are important to show command, just as they are in person. But don't pause too long, or your listeners will think you've had a stroke or—worse—lost interest.

Give everyone equal time in a conference call

If you're trying to achieve a sense of collaboration, then Feast and Pentland's research suggests that balance is important. Give everyone equal time. Make everyone *take* equal time; some slackers on the call may need to be prodded. And give them feedback to show that you acknowledge and appreciate what they've said. These are all practices you would do naturally in a face-to-face conversation (at least, I hope you would), but they become much harder to do virtually.

Finally, what about that weekly staff call? How can you make it better? The face-to-face standing meeting may have been a bit dull or routine, but at least there were people in the room. Necessary group bonding could happen effortlessly, and group solidarity could be maintained even if not much else went on.

On a virtual staff call, bonding is essentially nonexistent, and you should assume that all too many of the supposed participants are doing something else.

In addition to the above pointers that are relevant to your situation, begin by rethinking how long the meeting should go. Don't schedule it for a half-hour or an hour just because that's how long meetings went once upon a time. How about seven minutes? Or sixteen? Can you get everything done in that amount of time?

Next, set aside time when no one is allowed to do anything except socialize. The real point—one of them, at least—of regular staff meetings is to define and solidify the group for all participants. That happens not as much in the formal stuff as in the chitchat at the beginning and end. Make sure that there is real time for this essential work. And get everyone to participate.

If you've got a sense of fun, you might help establish rapport, at least initially, by having the group do entertaining social tasks like trivia, impromptu polls on current events, or contests that involve the whole group. Give out prizes. Make sure everyone participates. Pose a question for the next meeting such as "Come prepared to talk about your current pet or one you've owned in the past."

If the group is located in different regions and doesn't see each other face-to-face naturally, then *assign each person to do a thirty-second video on some social topic*—favorite food, favorite local spot, interesting local custom, and so on. The idea is to allow each participant to share with the group something about who and where the person is.

Finally, as you discuss items, and especially as you make decisions, poll the entire group. Never assume that silence implies consent. Silence can mean something in face-to-face meetings, because the leader can ascertain how people are feeling through their body language. But don't trust silence on a virtual call. Silence implies nothing but mute. Never forget that.

Make visible the rules and customs that are typically invisible in face-to-face settings

You might, for instance, say that the participants can offer comments for so long, and then follow this period with a feedback session where you deliberately go around the virtual room and ask everyone for a response. You need to keep the discussions shorter and routinely monitor the way people respond. Think of it as your job to be the referee of the conversation.

More than that, you need to ensure that emotions (normally revealed in body language) are verbalized when you sense that people feel strongly about something. You do this by checking with everyone around the room. Offering the participants a checklist of emotions can make it easier for people to share uncomfortable feelings when necessary. You can make it informal, by simply asking each person where he or she rates on an agreed-upon scale. For example, "On a one-to-five scale, where one is 'hate it' and five is 'I'm ecstatic,' how do you rate the new idea?" Or, "Rate the call (or idea, or decision, or proposed action) red, yellow, or green, where red is 'stop, I hate it,' yellow is 'OK, I have some concerns, but am ready to proceed cautiously', and green is 'I'm in.'"

For the longer term and for projects that last more than a month or two, establish a group activity with both virtual and physical aspects. For example, you might have everyone meet for virtual lunch and bring a national dish that people video and share. Or you might have participants take a tour of their office, floor, or building, either in real time or prepackaged. They can then share the resulting video with the rest of the team.

Combine the virtual and the real
for greatest effectiveness

The research in this area is in its infancy, but it shows that the combination of real and virtual becomes a powerful way to keep people engaged.[5] Thus, it's time to take it up a notch. Where teams used to go on whitewater rafting trips to build trust and to test their values, now you're going to engage your team in a shared activity, with part of the team owning the instructions for a puzzle and part of the team possessing the actual physical pieces of the puzzle to be put together. For example, you might give one part of the team a desirable electronic gadget that requires some assembly. Give the other part the instructions. Only in the combined effort will a successful solution be found. (And then, a month or two later, reverse the roles, so that no one becomes jealous.)

Remember that the virtual bottom line is that people on the other end of the phone are getting less information than they would if you were all together in person. That means that the format will always be inherently less interesting than an in-person meeting. It's an uphill battle to keep people's attention, check on whether they're still listening, and generally keep in touch. The following are some ways to keep the conversation engaging.

Smile when you talk. Smiling warms up your vocal tone. When you sit down, like most office workers do, for long periods, you tend not to breathe properly and you get lethargic. Fight that by going for a brisk walk before the call and then smiling during it.

Make the audioconference as interactive as possible. Conversations are interesting; listening to one person drone on for hours is not. Debates are interesting; monologues are not, unless you're

Richard III and your speechwriter is William Shakespeare. So, get two people in on the act.

Instead of a talk, make it an interview. If you've got a speaker scheduled or even if you don't, then consider employing the interview format rather than just having one person talk. The give-and-take of an interview is inherently interesting, especially if there are differing points of view.

Be clear and present about the logistics, timing, and duration. I'm not a big fan of agenda slides for in-person talks, but the aural equivalent is very helpful on a conference call. Announce how long you're going to run, announce frequently where you are, how long until questions, who's talking, who's on the phone, and so on. All of that helps create a more intimate feel, which would happen more or less automatically when everyone is together in the room. But it doesn't happen on the phone without help. Think of yourself as the play-by-play announcer for the show that is going on in the virtual space, and make it as exciting as the playoffs.

Use emotion-laden words when you're trying to communicate something important. Normally, we decode the intent, emotion, and attitudes of the speaker through body language and, to a lesser extent, through tone of voice. On the phone, you only get tone of voice, and the aural input is not very good at that, because the fidelity of telephones is notoriously bad. You have to work hard, therefore, to tell people how you feel; they won't necessarily pick it up from your body language unless you forgot to turn the video camera off.

Use words that label your emotions so that no one doubts how you feel. Say things like, "I'm excited," or "It's really sad that," or

"Wow, Jim, that's fantastic!" You'll feel like it's hard work until you practice it enough, but soon it will become second nature. And if you have teenage kids, the added benefit is that they'll think you're really, really weird when you start talking the same way at home.

Address the issue of dominance in conference calls

If you're the leader of the team, you need to ask yourself a key question: How much do you dominate the conversation on the conference call? How much do you *want* to dominate it? If you're like most people, and you like the sound of your own voice, the answer may be, "as much as possible."

But that attitude is not healthy for the team as a whole and especially not a virtual team. In the virtual world, a little goes a long way. Lacking the emotional connections that face-to-face body language provides, people are quicker to resent someone's dominating the conversation; they are quicker to decide that the person is a bad human being and are quicker to tune out. Thus, you have to think about how much influence you want to have—very carefully.

Let's begin with positional power. If you have lots of it, influence becomes a relatively simple proposition. People with power over others tend to talk more, to interrupt more, and to guide the conversation more, by picking the topics, for example. This power still works online, as long as everyone on the call knows who you are—and you don't abuse your power.

In the virtual space, your role as the convener of the meeting, the one who initiates the technology, gives you a certain added authority that entitles you to a little more positional power than you would normally have. People commonly begin a conference call by asking who called the meeting. Such issues are easily worked out through body language in person but need to be made vocal on a call. Don't overdo it, but if it's your meeting, you get to call the shots.

Now, what do you do if you want to challenge someone else's positional authority? A different kind of power is conveyed by passion for the subject at hand. The problem with passion in the virtual world is that it's mostly conveyed with body language, which is missing from the online configuration. As a result, passion can get filtered out and is less striking when it appears. Further, because people are tuned out online, they are less likely to notice your passion and respond to it in a virtual meeting.

On a conference call, then, you have to pour into your voice all the energy and passion that would normally get telegraphed when you jump up, start pacing around the room, and wave your hands in the air. Or when you pound on the table and raise your voice. Shouting doesn't convey the same punch on a phone call. It just annoys the listeners, who have to adjust their headsets.

Thus, passion can still carry the meeting in the virtual world, but just not quite as well. You have to be more articulate, muster more facts, tell better stories. The ante is raised on a call because the normal ways that passion sells itself—body language—are largely gone.

You can dominate the conversation, beating out positional power, if you have expertise. Asserting your expertise doesn't work quite as well virtually, but it still works much of the time. The diffident expert's voice will be lost online in the usual inefficiency of, say, a conference call, in the clamor of people wanting to be heard. Expertise without passion is not always effective, but if it's patient, it can be the last person standing in a debate and thereby get its turn.

Both passion without confidence and confidence without passion fail in the long run

Both online and in the real world, confidence all too often covers up a lack of expertise, and expertise without confidence can get ignored. It's the fate of the engineer with average or below-average communication skills.

And there's a final way to dominate a conference call: be the last to speak. The last person tends to carry the day, since everyone's input is less convincing, less forceful, and less authoritative than it is in person. If you can hold your verbal fire, do so—but don't wait too long. The other habit that gets magnified online, of course, is that people lose interest and move on. You don't want to wait until the verbal train has left the station to make your pitch.

We learn at a very early age that conversation is a pas de deux, a game that two (or more) people play. It involves breathing, winking, nodding, eye contact, head tilts, hand gestures, and a whole series of subtle nonverbal signals that help all the parties communicate with one another. All these signals drop out of the virtual world. Indeed, that's the whole problem in a nutshell: conversation is much less functional without these nonverbal signals. Conference calls inevitably involve far more interruptions, miscues, and cross-talking. We're not getting the signals we're used to getting to help us know when the other person is ready to hand the conversational baton on to us, and vice versa.

Audioconferences can work, as this case study shows

Given all the difficulties inherent in the medium of the conference call, can you base the success of a company on it? More and more often these days, teams include people who work remotely, spread out around the country or even around the world. But aviation consulting firm SimpliFlying has taken this new style of work to the extreme.[6] There are nine people at this small firm, and they're based in Singapore, India, Spain, Canada, and the United Kingdom. The company's headquarters are in Singapore, but the CEO is based in Canada and the team is entirely remote. "Everyone works from home," says Shashank Nigam, the CEO, "so we had to reinvent the way we do business." The conference call still has an essential role to play. But first, let's examine a little more how the company works virtually.

SimpliFlying doesn't function like a typical company. Employees can work whenever they want; there are no fixed hours. One of the consultants in Singapore is a night owl who likes to work at 2 a.m. Another consultant, based in Spain, makes time every evening to go out to dinner with friends. Most of the team members have been with the company for years, so they've come to understand how their colleagues like to work and when they'll typically be available. But the model allows for total flexibility. One of the Singapore-based consultants worked from Thailand for a week once. "She went to Thailand and lived in a treehouse for a week," Nigam says, "and all she needed was internet and she was able to do her work fine."

There are benefits to working on such a flexible, global team. "We are spread across every single time zone there is," Nigam says. That means they work on twenty-four-hour cycles. Singapore can start working on something, hand the project over to India when the Singapore workday is over, and then India can hand the work over to Europe. If Singapore starts work on a document during its workday, by the time Nigam is awake in Canada, the document has been through two drafts and is ready for him to review.

SimpliFlying accepts the good, the bad, and the beautiful

Of course, there are also significant challenges to being so spread out. "I have to be cognizant of the fact that my Europeans will go off to bed by the time it's noon here in Canada," Nigam says. The team players have very limited time available for real-time communication as a team—and of course, none of their communication happens face-to-face. Under these circumstances, "there's no such thing as brainstorming," Nigam says. It's just impossible to get the dynamic of people sitting around a whiteboard and sharing ideas if you're not in the same space.

SimpliFlying has taken an experimental approach to the challenges of working on an all-remote team. Some of the solutions are simple. For example, the company assigns two project managers to every client, so that there's always someone available, no matter where the client is based. Some solutions require more effort. The team meets up for in-person retreats three or four times a year. They'll typically rent an Airbnb accommodation and spend time doing the brainstorming they can't do on a conference call, as well as just spending time together, making up for all the watercooler chat they miss out on as a remote team.

And then there are the conference calls. Working on a remote team involves *a lot* of conference calls. That's a necessity. "Because we have very little face-to-face interaction in which all of us are together, we have daily stand-up calls," Nigam says. A daily meeting might seem like overkill for a traditional team, but for a remote team, it's crucial. "In a remote team, one of the most important things is to overcommunicate," Nigam says. "Unless we overcommunicate, things always slip between the cracks."

SimpliFlying does calls—but it does them differently

SimpliFlying's daily conference calls are designed to be more bearable than your typical conference call. First, they're strictly limited to ten to fifteen minutes. "It's very structured," Nigam says. "We will share what we've been up to in the last twenty-four hours, what we'll be up to in the next twenty-four hours, and what we need help on." With a team of nine people and at most fifteen minutes to talk, that means each update is just a minute or two. Everyone is forced to be clear and concise. "If we don't put a structure in place, people tend to ramble on," Nigam says. "We want to ensure that everyone has a chance to speak."

The daily stand-up meetings are "the backbone of our interaction," Nigam says. They're strictly focused on deadlines and key reminders for the rest of the team. "What we take off the call are any detailed discussions on project documents or client progress," he explains. Any more in-depth conversations are handled one-on-one or in small groups.

The SimpliFlying team has strict rules for one-on-one and small group calls as well. "No meeting can be longer than forty minutes," Nigam says. This rule started out as a limitation of Zoom, the software Nigam's group uses for video calls—Zoom's free product limits calls to forty minutes. But the external limitation soon became a huge benefit. "Hey, guess what," Nigam says. "If people only have forty minutes, they cut out the fluff and focus on what's most important." It's tough to concentrate on long calls, so SimpliFlying has eliminated them. The company enforces the same rules, very successfully, for client calls.

Time-limiting all meetings does mean that there's no time to waste. "When you are face-to-face, you can talk about the weather," Nigam says. "When you are on the phone, you don't talk about the weather. You cut to the chase." That's one reason why the regular staff retreats are so helpful—the team can get straight to business in their meetings because they've had plenty of chances to build relationships in person.

Both virtual and in-person interaction is important

The frequent phone calls and video calls require the team to be flexible and understanding with each other. "I'll be the first to admit, I do have two very young daughters, and I do work from home," Nigam says. "There have been times when my daughters have walked into my meeting." It helps that the team knows that he's working from home—and he's not trying to hide that fact. "I do the opposite of the BBC professor," he says. The professor's interview on BBC went viral when his kids came into the room where he was doing the interview remotely. Instead of trying to shoo the kids away, as the professor did, Nigam will take them onto his lap and have them say hi. Acknowledging the interruption works better than trying to pretend it isn't happening.

"All of these rules together have worked quite well for us," Nigam says. And the team is still open to experimenting. The mandatory vacation policy has only been around for a year, and the "deep work" Fridays are just a couple of months old. Making a global, 24-7 team work is a challenge, but SimpliFlying is determined to make it work.

Practical fix

The audioconference cheat sheet

- Put some life into your voice. Smile when you talk.

- Put someone else in charge.

- Put a limit on the formal remarks; make the audio-conference as interactive as possible.

- Add an advocate on your side for the other side if there are two sides.

- Circulate an agenda in advance and appoint someone to take notes and send them out to all parties afterward.

- Take on or appoint the role of active listener. This person should report back to the group often.

- Rethink how long the meeting should go.

- Set aside time when no one is allowed to do anything except socialize.

- Assign each person to do a thirty-second video or report of some kind on some social topic.

- Poll the entire group when making decisions that affect everyone.

- Make visible and actual any rules, customs, or courtesies that are typically left invisible in a face-to-face setting.

- Establish a group activity with both virtual and physical aspects.

- Combine the virtual and the real for greatest effectiveness.

- Instead of a talk, make it an interview.

- Be clear and present about the logistics, timing, and duration of the meeting.

- Use emotion-laden words when you're trying to communicate something important.

- Be aware of your power and position, and use both appropriately.

CHAPTER SUMMARY

- There are three kinds of conference calls; vary your approach accordingly.

- Keep public calls short, and appoint an MC.

- Keep team and client calls on track, and strive for balance.

- Keep weekly update calls focused, and avoid chitchat.

- Vary the format and the participants.

- Become aware of the relationship between power and influence on the call.

- One company, SimpliFlying, provides an innovative model for making conference calls effective.

THE WEBINAR

When Steve Jobs first presented the iPhone to the world, he said it was revolutionary. He was both right and wrong. He was right in that the iPhone has changed our lives in more ways than just about any other device introduced in my lifetime and yours, but he was wrong in a crucial way: he didn't understand what it was for, at least completely. He introduced it as a combination of already existing things—the phone, the iPod, and a browser. He was only right about one of those three.

The way people use the iPhone (and other smartphones) is indeed primarily as a browser—the last function on Jobs's list. According to recent research by Pew, eight in ten Americans own a smartphone, and 93 percent of them use it to access the internet at least weekly.[1] The pattern is similar around the world. That means that an extraordinary half of all internet use is now taking place on mobile phones.

But the next two most common things to do on your cell phone are to take videos and pictures (seven in ten do so weekly) and to text (two-thirds do so weekly).

Jobs can be forgiven for thinking like most of humanity about his revolutionary device. Most of us imagine that the future will be an extension of the past. We can make guesses, to be sure, about flying cars and teleporting, but we miss the real transformation that inventions like the iPhone create, because it is so hard to imagine real change.

Information is not as asymmetrical as it used to be

Before the mobile phone, checking up on people was sometimes difficult. The question "What's happening to so-and-so?" used to be potentially fraught with great meaning and misery. Today, the most common response to the question is, "I don't know; shoot her a text."

We use Jobs's invention to allow us to connect in new and interesting ways with our friends, family, acquaintances, business colleagues, customers, and others. The most basic human need is being satisfied by the communication device we now can carry in our pockets and operate anywhere with a thumb or another finger or two.

Here's the essential point: mobile devices enable overwhelmingly one-to-one or one-to-several communication. Sometimes it's a shout-out to your whole tribe, but most of the time, it's one-to-one or one person to a handful. We rarely use these devices for one-to-many communication. Why? We don't favor it unless we've elevated the person doling out the communication to a high level. We don't mind being in the audience if the speaker is a famous actor or politician. But if we've never heard of the person, the appeal is minimal.

Let's examine this truly awful way to communicate

Add to these disadvantages the colder, less emotional digital forms of one-to-many communications, and you have a truly awful way to communicate.

That's the webinar.

Webinars, for most people, are a form of torture. Participants sign up because of some interest in the topic or the speaker, but quickly find that the information is sparse and the selling component heavy. Or the speaker is terrible and the slides worse and it's just impossible to get much from the hour despite your best intentions.

I give webinars a separate chapter because they're so awful. Even though the technology is similar to the conference call, the webinar is worse. Why? It's not a conversation, like something you can have with someone you love on your mobile phone via voice, text, or pictures. The webinar is simply a disembodied voice from a relative stranger, emotions stripped out, leaking out of a computer or phone. Or worse—a computer phone.

What makes a speaker memorable is emotion—literally, since memory works through emotion. Put even a great speaker on a webinar, and most of the emotion is stripped out by the bandwidth reduction of the technology. The result? Boredom. Nails-in-the-forehead boredom. Jump-off-a-bridge boredom.

Add video, and curiously, things don't get much better. It's time for some tough love on running effective, engaging webinars, whether the picture is there or not. (I'll talk in more detail about video conversations in the next chapter.)

We have too many meetings and way too many webinars

In-person meetings are the bane of the working world. Most managers complain that they have to attend far too many meetings with way too little purpose. And yet we can't get along without them.

What are their primary faults? Why do we hate them so much? They don't start on time, there is no agenda, or the one that has been presented isn't followed anyway. No one documents the results, if there are any, and there's often no follow-up. Add mobile phones to the mix, and half the group is only half present, regularly sneaking semi-surreptitious glances at their phones in a desperate attempt to keep up with the steady stream of additions to their to-do lists.

But at least they're all sitting in the same room. As readers will be aware of by now, even if the participants aren't looking at each other, they are exchanging emotion, intent, attitude, and decisions through their unconscious minds. A virtual meeting robs the participants of that rich and important source of emotion, information, and connection.

A one-to-many webinar is even worse, because you have less reason to engage in the first place. Your unconscious never gets anything interesting or important from the deracinated voice on the speakerphone or in your earbuds, your emotions are left out of the event, and all the senses except the auditory are effectively put into storage for the duration. In the end, then, a webinar takes everything potentially bad about face-to-face meetings, doubles down on these things, and adds a few more truly crucial soul-destroying challenges to the mix for good measure.

Here's a possible solution: *don't do them.*

"But wait," you say. "We couldn't possibly communicate with the large numbers of people we reach, in the personal, live way that we do, without webinars. You're being foolish. We would be stupid to stop doing them. And they're almost free!"

A radical suggestion: don't do webinars

With that last imagined argument, you've hit on the real reason that people do webinars. They're a cheap form of meeting. No one has to leave home or the office. No one has to commit to the experience—people can drop off if the webinar doesn't grab them. Heck, attendees don't even have to get dressed if they don't want to.

On the internet, no one knows you're wearing pajamas.

We humans crave collaborative experiences, but there are simply too many obstacles in the way of a webinar for it to have much of a chance of becoming a collaborative experience. So how can you take this miserable form of communications—one that violates almost everything that's important about the attributes of good communications that people need for them to be successful—and make it work? Following are several suggestions for making webinars better. Don't say you didn't know—henceforth. There is no plausible deniability where webinars are concerned.

First of all, practice good online meeting hygiene

Good organizational structure of the webinar can show the attendees that you take their time seriously. The following practices are good ways to show people that you value them and have set high expectations for the webinar.

Start on time. This recommendation sounds obvious, and it should be, but I've participated in a number of webinars that were run by good companies but that didn't start on time because people are still signing in at five minutes past—and ten minutes past. To start on time, you need to begin the tech setup thirty minutes beforehand and then be ready to be ruthless when the hour comes. Just start, and don't try to catch people up by repeating, starting again, and so on. Catch-up like this penalizes the people who did start on time. And it creates an awful herky-jerky opening: "Oh, I hear someone else has joined.

Where are you from? Who is that? Let's get started. Oh, there's someone else . . ."

Have an agenda, and stick to it. Sticking to an agenda is a challenge for me, personally, because I get carried away with the topic, with listener questions, and so on, and cheerfully get lost in the weeds of communications debating some fine point with my interlocutors. To address this particular failing of mine, I've taken assigning someone else the job of timekeeper, with strict instructions to keep us all on track. The right to interrupt must be given, and given verbally, or else the hapless timekeeper will be polite and wait.

Have a buddy, or better yet, have two. You need a partner to help pick up the points that have been dropped—questions that get forgotten or points left unsaid—in the conversation. And you need someone else to run the tech. I once participated in a webinar through one of those cheap-and-cheerful free online webinar companies, and the two of us running the call were also presenting. We had no one to help with the tech. So, of course, a few minutes in, a terrible howl of feedback developed. No one had any idea where it was coming from, but it sure made the webinar excruciating. With a tech person, we might have figured it out or suggested an alternative.

Never go more than ten minutes without some kind of break and change. Stop for a check-in, for questions, for everyone to howl at the moon—anything to break up the monotony. Questions are particularly helpful. They'll help you gauge how everyone is doing.

Announce time points to your audience. Either you or your buddy should regularly comment on what the status of the meeting is. "Great, Nick. We've been going ten minutes, so it's time for a break. We'll take questions for five minutes, and then we have two more segments of twenty minutes each. Is everyone OK with that?" Imagine you're doing color commentary for a ball game.

Second, strengthen the human and digital connections

Put the emotions back in that the format takes out. This is the most important and toughest rule of the road for webinar devotees. If you insist on doing webinars, then you must figure out how to consciously restore emotion in these sessions. The simplest way is to begin to train yourself to add in emotional words that we normally leave out of conversation because how we feel is obvious from our body language. "I'm concerned," "I'm thrilled," "That comment really upsets me because ..." Tell your audience how you feel. If you don't, how will they know? Remember, your voice won't signal your emotions accurately or much.

Set up ground rules for collaboration. Because people crave conversation and collaboration, make it easy for them to do both. Create some rules, announce them, and stick to them. You might take questions every ten minutes. You should set up several channels—texting, emails, and so on—for people to use in the webinar chat room so that everyone's questions can get answered. For my previous book, also published by Harvard, I was the speaker for a webinar that had six thousand listeners.

Once Harvard and I knew that the number was so big, we decided to take as many questions as we could, and then I asked everyone who still had questions to send me an email. After the webinar, I answered all these emails.

Keep the focus. Stick to one topic, and explore that. Don't branch out to other things just because you're interested in them. If people ask unrelated questions, compliment the question and mention that because it lies outside the scope of the webinar, you'd be happy to answer it in an email. Share what you can beforehand to make the webinar as focused and as efficient as you can. It's amazing how few companies do this effectively. Set up a website. Include whatever material you think will help people prepare.

And follow up with something after the fact. Have a book, an ebook, or a pdf to give away. Make it appropriate for your audience.

Begin with a compelling story. There's simply no substitute for good storytelling to engage people.

Be clear whether your meeting is about an exchange of information or decision making. There's a trend among publicly traded companies to offer their annual meetings as virtual-only meetings. Virtual has the advantage of allowing more people to attend, especially those who have insufficient money or time to make the trip to corporate headquarters. But it also muddies the waters around matters like vote taking, approving the slate of directors, and sharing the company's financial health and prospects. These kinds of meetings will no doubt eventually go away altogether, because the inferior, virtual version will appeal less and less and ultimately not seem worth the effort to anyone.

Appoint someone to be the recording secretary if there are issues to be decided. The recording role is less important if the avowed purpose of the meeting is simply information sharing, but it still might be done. You need a recorder if the meeting is a decision-making one. A summary of whatever transpired should be published (online) for all the participants—and those unable to make the session—to access.

If there are follow-ups to do, note those too, and notify those affected, especially if, during the meeting, the speaker agrees to do something. This means of keeping track is important to maintain or enhance the integrity of the speaker and conveners of the webinar. Especially in public webinars, but in fact in all such meetings, promises made should be kept.

Limit the number of participants. For a decision-making meeting, the research suggests that five to seven is the optimal number of people to attend.[2] Webinars are, of course, typically intended to accommodate many more people than that. Some organizations use webinars to generate income, charging for seats. In that case, their profit motive would suggest no upper limit to the participants, beyond any technical limitations.

Nonetheless, there is an advantage, too, in exclusivity and scarcity. As an alternative, I recommend limiting the number to *Dunbar's number*, or somewhere around 150, which is, according to anthropologist Robin Dunbar, the upper limit of human relationships that we can apparently sustain.[3] This limit creates the impression that you're joining a tribe, not a rabble, and the psychological benefits will redound not only to the participants but also to the conveners as well, since everyone will perceive that a human connection is at least possible.

Have an overarching story line to your webinar. You'll be breaking up your content into chapters of ten minutes each, but don't take these discrete chunks as license to connect a few ideas together loosely. You owe your audience a story arc.

Summarize at the end of each chapter and tease the next one. Think Dan Brown. Tell the audience members what they've learned and intrigue them with the possibilities of what's coming next.

Vary the content and form of those chapters. Keep the variety coming. You might do one section as a Q and A, another as an interview, a third as a rant, and so on. Don't make every chapter what all too many entire webinars consist of: a middle-aged male voice talking tonelessly about how to revolutionize your sales force.

In general, keep things a little more formal than a face-to-face meeting. In person, informality can be charming, because we can see and feel that the speaker knows what he or she is talking about. Over the phone, informality is baffling and off-putting.

Third, get the whole group involved

You might say, for example, "We are going to stop every ten minutes and call out each locale to give you a chance to ask questions." You decide the format, but do provide some means for group involvement.

Then, keep track of those who don't participate, and give them a chance to do so on the penultimate break. Don't take this action on the last break, because people tend to remember the last thing they hear, and you don't want to make nonparticipation the most memorable thing about your webinar. But do call out—or offer the opportunity, depending on the meeting and its ground rules—to nonparticipants so that they can respond.

Do go over the ground rules at the beginning. You can also publish the rules on the site associated with the webinar, but you have no guarantee that anyone will read them, so it's essential to go over the rules as you begin. The rules should include guidelines on mute buttons, questions, and timing.

Before you get to the meat of the presentation, go over expectations. You might mention the purpose and point of the occasion, the goals, or the context that you think is appropriate.

Don't forget to announce who is on the call. You can do this in whatever way tact recommends, but remember that the sweetest sound of all, as Dale Carnegie was fond of saying, is the sound of someone saying your name.

And regularly use active listening to restate questions for clarity and agreement. "So what I hear you saying is X. Is that correct?" Get agreement before continuing.

Also, summarize regularly. As noted above, you might do so at the end of each ten-minute segment or even more often. At the end, you'll want to give a further summation, suggest the next steps if there are any, and thank the participants.

Fourth, use the media and the technology available to you

If it's a public conference, then encourage the use of Twitter and other social media channels. Provide the necessary hashtags and other information so that everyone will comment in the same channel and stream and you can monitor the flow. A recent study at the University of Leicester found that speakers at a medical conference were monitoring their Twitter feeds in real time and reacting to the comments they saw on that channel.[4] The result was mixed; some of the tweets were negative and highly distracting for the speakers. These findings underscore my earlier recommendation for a buddy to help with this sort of running commentary.

Just like face-to-face conferences, webinars should have backup speakers ready. If the show must indeed go on, then you need to be prepared should the scheduled speaker be unable to speak for one reason or another. The backup speaker is rarely called on, but is essential nonetheless.

And back up everything else. Technology is more and more reliable but still can fall apart when you would least like it to. Have two of everything ready to go.

And finally, consider adding music to your webinar. Think of this as a form of sonic branding and an opportunity for inducing emotional responses. Because music is a shortcut to an emotional experience, it is a very good way to restore the emotion that a benighted technology has removed.

David Meerman Scott, a successful speaker and the author of the perennial best seller *The New Rules of Marketing and PR*, currently on its sixth edition, has launched a company to provide speakers and webinar leaders with signature music that they can own and use to create musical connections to their webinars. He calls it sonic branding, and the company is called Signature Tones. The result could significantly add emotion and interest back into the format, which so notoriously lacks these qualities.[5]

Take some further tips from a webinar pro

Roger Courville knows that most people hate webinars.[6] He has been in the business of studying and improving the form since 1999, and he has seen the technology change over the years. "What I discovered," he says, "was that it wasn't about technology per se. It was about communication." Courville soon came to believe that there was a real value proposition behind webinars—that, while they couldn't replace an in-person presentation, they had some value above and beyond a phone call. "There was a very real way to help people connect and communicate," Courville says. The question was, what exactly was different about this new form of communication? After all, as Courville points out, "the medium through which we communicate always transforms the experience."

Courville believes that the way people approach new technologies like webinars colors the way they use those technologies. "We tend to evaluate new situations based on old information," Courville says. "It's part of why people resist change so significantly." When it comes to webinars, people tend to notice what they lose compared with an in-person presentation, rather than focusing on the unique strengths of the format, Courville says.

Unfortunately, the way most people approach webinars does make this format a pale imitation of in-person presentation, Courville says. "The default is that [the webinars] keep the worst parts of the in-person presentation" and lose the best parts, he says. Most people don't bother to push past that first impression of what's possible in a webinar and discover the medium's unique strengths. "There are things you can do better in virtual presentations, but often people stop before they get to that discovery," Courville says.

Beware the Uncle Joe problem

Courville calls it "the Uncle Joe problem." Imagine you want to learn how to play golf. You know that Uncle Joe plays golf, so you go out with him to try to learn. Only Uncle Joe is terrible at golf; you just don't know enough to know it. "The vast majority of people now have attended webinars," Courville says, "which means that they've attended bad ones." This modeling of bad habits often starts with webinar companies themselves. They use webinars for marketing and lead generation. They use a simple format, talking over PowerPoint slides for forty-five minutes and then taking questions. As a result, far too many people think that this format is the only way to do webinars, Courville says. "If you open up Microsoft Word, do you think there is only one way to write?" he says. "And yet we do webinars, and we think there's only one way to present or communicate."

Perhaps because so many webinars are so dull, the trends in how audiences receive them are not encouraging for presenters. The ratio of registrants to actual attendees is getting worse, Courville says. It's now common for a hundred people to sign up for a webinar and only thirty or forty to show up. Why? Most webinars aren't very interactive, and people have figured out that it's more efficient to play the recording back later, so they can rewind and fast-forward and absorb the information at their own pace. "If you are purely consuming information, consuming it in an on-demand format is a more effective way," Courville says.

Asking people to show up at a specific time and spend an hour with you is asking a lot of your audience, Courville notes. "If your webinar is the same psychosocial experience as watching a YouTube video, and it would actually be easier for your audience to watch a YouTube video, you are charging too much," he says. You're asking more of your audience than you're giving back, he explains.

Understand the true meaning of a webinar

So, what's the answer? Courville believes that the quest for better webinars starts with realizing what a webinar really is. "If you're using a real-time medium, take advantage of things that are uniquely real time," Courville says. "Plan to connect and communicate with your audience."

Courville lays out a simple framework for how to approach a webinar to take full advantage of what the medium offers: analyze, map, and discover. First, he says, "analyze what you do in person." When you do an in-person presentation, how do you like to be introduced? Do you use handouts? How do you handle formal and informal audience interactions? Don't just think about the main body of the presentation; take the whole experience into account.

Too many webinars are built on the assumption that the audience will sit passively and absorb the content for an hour or even longer. "Are there are any other contexts where you would sit passively and watch content for two or three hours?" Courville asks. "Yes, it's called *The Lord of the Rings*." Assuming you're not movie producer Peter Jackson and your webinar isn't as engaging as a Hollywood blockbuster, it's probably best to try to build in some interactivity. If you don't, you're not taking full advantage of this real-time communication tool.

The second step in Courville's planning process is to map the different types of interactions to the tools offered in your webinar software. "Some things are going to translate," Courville says. "Some things are not going to translate. Some things can be adapted, and you find a different way to achieve the same objective."

If you like to interact with your audience a lot in person, look for ways to interact online. For example, a good presenter listens to the audience—and most webinar software now includes tools that allow you to virtually listen and check in on how your audience is doing. Many platforms now offer attention meters that will tell you how many people have clicked into another window. You can also ask questions or take a poll to check that people are understanding your material.

Always be responding

A good webinar presenter should respond to questions throughout a presentation, Courville says. Audience members can type in questions through most webinar software. Responding right away will show that you want to connect with them, not just give them a data dump. Most software also now allows presenters to create breakout groups. With the click of a button, you can organize the audience into smaller groups, with each group placed into a video chat. This capability is a great way to break up a longer webinar and help the audience master your material.

The third and final step in Courville's process is to discover what you can do online that you can't do offline. Every communication medium has its own unique strengths, and webinars are no exception. Say that in a typical workshop session, you would have participants go around and introduce themselves. That might take fifteen minutes in person. But if you have participants in a webinar type in their introductions simultaneously, it only takes a minute or two, saving you time to dig deeper into the material.

The technology exists to make webinars engaging, interactive, and worth your audience's time. It's just that most people don't know enough about the software they're using, Courville says. "They are just used to doing things in a poor way, and they don't know any better." The good news is that the underused capacity of the software means there's plenty of room to blow your audience away with a few simple improvements to the typical approach. "The bar is so low," Courville says, "there are a lot of wins to be had."

Offer your audience creative value

Besides the webinar content itself, there are creative ways you can reward the participants. Consider these suggestions.

Connect the webinar to the news of the day in some way. Potential participants will ask why they should attend a webinar, and you need to have an answer. But if you can also answer the other part of the question, "Why now?," you can greatly increase participation. Timeliness is powerful.

Offer something unexpected near the end of the webinar. Surprises can delight audiences and keep them hanging on for more. They are a way to make a humdrum webinar experience unforgettable.

Offer face-to-face meetings for a select few. You can do this either before or after the fact. You might, for example, offer to the first few signups a free ticket to fly to the studio where the webinar is being recorded. This step has the added advantage of providing a live audience for the speaker, and it's fun to see behind the scenes. Get those participants to help with the visual social media.

Don't stop when the webinar is done

Finally, here are a few pointers to follow after the webinar is done. If you want to increase the likelihood that your webinar will defy expectations, logic, and the unhappy history of most webinars and *actually be remembered*, then consider taking the following postwebinar actions.

Use social media to create a winner after the fact. George Bernard Shaw, when he was a young, unknown, impoverished, and struggling playwright, wrote glowing reviews of his own plays and published them under assumed names in the journals of the day. He was using the social media of his day astutely, and you can too—provided, of course, that you find real people from the webinar to say the nice things. In this transparent era, don't try to practice Shaw's deception. You might get caught, and anyway, as President Nixon famously said in a slightly different context, "It would be wrong."

Think about creating short videos before and after your webinar. Just because you're virtual doesn't mean that you can't video the speaker and put out the results on social media. People connect with other people's faces, especially on video, so videos can be a powerful way to increase interest.

Start an online discussion about the knowledge and insights developed in the webinar. The webinar provides the hook and the headline; it's up to you to keep the conversation going. You're going to have to feed it, at least to get it started, but if you can keep it engaging, you may well begin something with lasting value.

Crowdsource everything. Follow up the webinar with polls, surveys, prizes for participation, and so on. If you make it fun, people will participate.

Give away things that will increase retention and participation. For example, you might offer a follow-up coaching session or one-on-one call with the speaker. That kind of connection is precisely what's missing in the one-to-many form that is the webinar.

Offer smaller discussion sessions to participants after the webinar is over. These sessions can be with the speaker or other representatives from the organization. Small discussion groups can create a sense of insider exclusivity that is appealing to many participants.

Periodically send follow-up items of value to participants. You can send further information inexpensively via pdf and email, but physical objects, such as letters, printed reports, and photographs, have a charm and solidity that virtual objects don't. Take advantage of the real world as much as possible in the virtual.

As these examples show, there are many ways to spice up a webinar, and not all of them need to take place during the webinar itself.

In the end, webinar leaders need to communicate with intent, just like any other speaker or leader who needs to make the right impression on the audience. Much of what is successful body language in person falls short online; that's a central tenet of this book. But even in the lowly webinar, you can use some of the techniques that work much better in person.

For example, one way to increase the likelihood and speed of building trust is to mirror the other person you're meeting or getting to know. It's a phenomenon well studied in the body-language world. We see lovers, longtime friends, and coworkers who agree on something unconsciously mirroring each other on a minute-by-minute basis. It's our bodies' way of telling the other person, "Hey, we're alike, we agree, we're on the same page here."

You can consciously mirror the relative stranger in front of you and thereby greatly increase both the depth and the rate of trust building. It needs to be done with some subtlety and care, but it's rare that the other person will notice unless you become hyperactive in your efforts and try to mirror every little twitch. Less is more.

Online, via voice, all you can do is mirror the other person's speech patterns, tone, and manner of speaking as much as possible. If a participant asks a question in a rapid-fire way, for example, you can respond in that way. Or if you hear a questioner using certain phrases, play those phrases back to him or her. Of course, using the name of your participant is gratifying for the person and increases trust. The palette is more limited in voice-only interaction, but the intent is the same.

The conscious study and use of body language for specific psychological purposes is demanding work, but the payoff is rich in stronger connections with the rest of the human race. And that goes for webinar speakers, too.

Practical fix

The webinar cheat sheet

Use these suggestions to move beyond the mediocre expectations usually afforded the webinar.

1. Share what you can beforehand to make the webinar as focused and as efficient as you can.

2. Think about creating short videos before and after your webinar.

3. Just as in a face-to-face conference, webinars should have backup speakers ready.

4. You should also back up everything else.

5. Consider adding music to your webinar.

6. Limit the number of participants.

7. Have a buddy or, better yet, have two.

8. Start on time.

9. Have an agenda, and stick to it.

10. Announce who is on the call.

11. Because people crave conversation and collaboration, make it easy for them to do both. Create some rules, announce them, and stick to them.

12. Announce a way to involve the whole group, and periodically use this approach.

13. Be clear on whether your meeting is about an exchange of information or decision making.

14. Have an overarching story line to your webinar.

15. Appoint someone to be the recording secretary, if there are things to be decided.

16. Before the start of the meat of the presentation, go over expectations.

17. Never go more than ten minutes without some kind of break and change.

18. Either you or your buddy should regularly comment on what the status of the meeting is.

19. Put back into the webinar the emotions that the virtual format takes out.

20. Keep the focus.

21. Follow up with something valuable after the fact.

22. Summarize at the end of each chapter, or part, of the webinar, and provide a tease for the next one.

23. Vary the content and format of those chapters.

24. In general, keep things a little more formal than in a face-to-face meeting.

25. Keep track of those who don't participate, and give them a chance to do so on the penultimate break.

26. Regularly use active listening to restate questions for clarity and agreement.

27. If it's a public conference, then encourage the use of Twitter and other social media channels.

28. If there are follow-ups to do, note those too, and notify those affected.

29. Use social media to create a winner after the fact.

30. Start an online discussion about the knowledge and insights developed in the webinar.

31. Crowdsource everything.

32. Connect the webinar to the news of the day in some way.

33. Give away things that will increase retention and participation.

34. Offer something unexpected near the end of the webinar.

35. Offer smaller discussion sessions to participants after the webinar.

36. Periodically send follow-up items of value to participants.

37. Offer face-to-face meetings for a select few.

CHAPTER SUMMARY

- Webinars are a miserable form of communication; figure out ways to make them better.

THE CHAT SESSION

Pity poor Robert Kelly, professor of political science at Pusan National University in South Korea.[1] He was mid-interview with the BBC, on March 10, 2017, just after 8:00 p.m. his time, talking about the desperately important issue of the first impeachment of a South Korean head of government. The interview was being conducted live from his home office. Kelly was nicely done up in a suit and tie, hair combed, a serious-looking wall map of the world in the background, when first one of his kids, then another, burst into the room and starting heading for Daddy. Seconds later, his harried wife scrambles in, scoops up both kids, and hurries out, trying her best to be invisible. The video clip went viral, naturally, and gave us all a good laugh and made Kelly temporarily famous.

The bit was funny for the world and embarrassing for Kelly because it mixed two worlds in the unforgiving light of a Skype linkup—the BBC and Kelly's kids. And because he did his best to push his child out of the way. His failure to do so only added to the fun.

We debate endlessly the problems of our 24-7 existence and bemoan the intrusion of email and conference calls into our nonwork hours, but adding video to the mix creates another potential level of intrusion. One kind of mixing of those worlds, work and home, causes stress and must be managed, but the next level, which Kelly experienced, means crisis. Fortunately, in his case the world decided to laugh and move on, but he will long be known not as "Professor Kelly, expert," but as "Professor Kelly, that guy whose kids interrupted his BBC interview." Both sobriquets have their charms, but the latter is not consequence-free.

Balance is gone; *blend* is in

So thoroughly have the intrusions of the digital world disrupted our old, pre-twenty-first-century existences that many people no longer talk about work-life balance. Instead, it's fashionable to talk about work-life *blend*. Which basically means that you're giving up on balance. You do one to the extreme, perhaps, and then the other. The problem is that most of those blends involve taking the phone with you to the game, or some other similar sort of ugly compromise.

Video makes it much harder to blend. As Robert Kelly found out. A little background noise on a phone hookup would have been a different thing, wouldn't it? No interruption to speak of, and no viral video.

So why is video different? A naive response would say, "Video is different because it's like being there in person. You can see and hear. What else do you need?" According to this line of reasoning, of your basic five senses, sight and sound are by far the most important. Taste, touch, and smell only confirm what you're seeing and hearing.

But video turns out to be far more complicated than that. Some companies have set up expensive whole-room videoconferencing facilities with half of a conference room in one location and the other half in some other place. When you dial up

Shanghai, then, you get a complete conference table, sort of, and a group of people sitting around it as if they were all in the same room.

Almost there is almost not-there

Indeed, for brief periods the setup almost works like that. Then someone moves, and they're cut off from your view, but your brain is telling you that you should be able to see them. That's curiously stressful. Why should it be?

For answers, I turned to John Medina, developmental molecular biologist, director of the Brain Center for Applied Learning Research at Seattle Pacific University, and author of the celebrated book *Brain Rules*.[2] Medina explains, "The brain gets inputs from many sources. When one of those channels is missing, it makes things up to fill the gap. And it gets stressed." He adds, "The brain basically doesn't know what to do with virtual visual images, because they lack a host of inputs we would get in person, like changes in air pressure and so on, so it responds by getting stressed-out."

Medina notes that the brain gets used to a certain level of errors and omissions in virtual exchanges like phone calls, webinars, and videoconferences, but it isn't happy with the impoverished picture it's receiving. So, it "builds up a spreadsheet of responses from past experiences, because the brain is ridiculously adaptable, like starting to see all caps in email and texting as shouting." But the whole process remains both stressful and unsatisfying for the brain.

In Medina's taxonomy, email is the worst, the most impoverished. Following that is the phone. And only a little better is video. When I asked him what he suggested to ameliorate each of these impoverished channels, he suggested that the best thing to do with an email is "call the other person up and read the email to them." At least, in that way, you'd have a chance to ask the question "How did what I just said make you feel?" This key question is, in a very real sense, the question we always want answered as humans most urgently: What is that other person's intent toward me? We are hardwired, as Medina points out in *Brain Rules*, to ask basic questions on meeting other people, questions like "Is this person a friend or foe?" Not getting clear answers for those kinds of basic questions makes our brains very nervous.

How are you feeling right now?

For phone conferences and webinars, Medina notes, "Virtually all group social signal is absent. There is no good fix for that." And for video? "A little better but still very stressful," he says. He recommends instituting the perception check outlined above. "How did what I said just now make you feel?"

Adding almost any kind of emotional connection in the virtual world helps. Indeed, a study of virtual negotiations found that brief discussions of social connections like hobbies greatly increased the likelihood of the negotiation's ultimate success.[3]

There are a few basic rules you have to understand if you're going to use Skype or something like it. Let's consider them next.

You don't have to shout

You do have to be more aware of the conversational handoffs in virtual interactions than in a face-to-face discussion. Many of the little signals that tell us how to conduct a conversation, with the appropriate opportunities for the other person or people to chime in, don't translate even in the video world. For example, we need our full peripheral vision to make a conversation work, and the two-dimensional screen makes such vision much more difficult.

Follow some commonsense rules when using Skype

The first rule of Skype is an old-fashioned one. Create some formal, but simple, mechanism for handing off the conversation to the next participant—such as a hand raise. The discipline required takes some people a little time to learn, but the results in terms of increased clarity are worth it.

Second, you absolutely must provide an agenda for a Skype call that's going to last more than ten minutes. And adhere to it. Third, because people are often too polite to want to express problems of communication on their end, you always should begin with a check-in around the Skype circle to establish local issues that might affect the call, questions of timing, and so on.

One company that has three offices in different cities relies on a mix of conference calls, videoconferencing, face-to-face meetings, instant messaging, and emails to conduct daily business. The company reports difficulty with a number of these channels, but videoconferencing may be the most difficult—simply because it is the newest communication channel still in the business world and employees have less experience with it.

As this organization finds, it's hard for participants to know when to speak. It can feel quite rude to interrupt, and yet if you don't, you may in essence disappear because a two-dimensional picture is not the same to our brains as a real person. The other participants may forget that you're there unless you assert yourself from time to time. And yet doing so can feel arbitrary, clumsy, or overly aggressive.

This company reports that, in its meetings, its employees often feel compelled to add something on every point to counteract the feeling of invisibility. The result is meetings that seem to last forever.

At the same time, where there are real disagreements, employees can feel more constrained in a virtual meeting and might hold their negative comments until they have a chance for a one-to-one conversation later. The result is yet more meetings and inefficiency.

We don't say what we mean on video, and we don't feel heard

Employees also feel intense pressure to keep up with the email and Slack conversations endlessly swirling around them. If they do keep up, it is at the peril of not getting anything else done. If they don't keep up, then other employees can feel slighted.

Then there are the meetings that are mixed with in-person people and virtual people. The virtual participants feel like second-class citizens and routinely fail to get heard—or to feel heard. These problems with modern virtual and digital ways of working are endemic, and the solutions to them involve learning new ways of working that can feel awkward and intrusive at first.

There are three broad categories of response necessary, and each category has applications for the videoconference. First, you need to institute formal means for turn-taking. Second, you need to create a new role, that of an MC, to provide a referee and coach for the various forms of virtual meetings, to ensure that all participants feel heard. And third, you need a way to do what Medina calls *perception checks* to understand the emotional undercurrents hidden by the virtual nature of the conversation or meeting.

These three broad categories cover the elements missing from virtual conversations and meetings. Let's look at how they apply to the videoconference.

Taking turns is less automatic online

Turn-taking is surprisingly difficult to master once we humans are taken out of our normal settings, where it's a natural part of conversing, such as sitting around a campfire, munching on the marrow bones of woolly mammoths, and talking over the hunt. As we grow up, we learn a whole retinue of winks, blinks, eye rolls, nods, head tilts, and so on that help regulate simple conversation. We gradually extend those to more-formal settings in classrooms and workplaces, and by the time we're adults, most of us can take turns without having to think consciously about it very much.

In a video setting, a whole set of other sensory perceptions beyond mere sight and sound is missing. I've alluded to the differences in air movement caused by the shifting in space of the people around us. In addition, we rely on a complete mental map of the room we're in to keep track of the people near us; on video, that mental mapping is hampered, so we don't know where exactly the potential friends and foes in the room are located. That's stressful.

Lacking many of these clues, our brains get busy trying to make up information, and we have a harder time getting accurate signals from the few sensory inputs that are left. And so we find it hard to get a grip on the normal activities of turn-taking. We need help.

A simple technique is to first discuss and then implement the device of hand raising. It's familiar to just about everyone from school, and it is minimally intrusive. Get verbal agreement from everyone (in turn) to wrap up what they're saying when they see a hand go up, and the problem is solved, for the most part.

An MC's role can be as involved as you want

When there are more than two participants, institute the role of an MC, or a chair. The chair's responsibility is to keep track of the discussion at a level the group is comfortable with and to ensure that everyone's voice is heard. If he or she is able, the MC can also help you summarize points, compare people's points of view, note actions to be taken, ensure that the agenda is adhered to, and do any other task to help keep the meeting on target. The MC can also help with the third area, below.

Conduct a perception check

The third area, then, is Medina's perception check. As I noted in chapter 7, the best method is the simplest. Have each participant rate his or her emotional temperature in three categories—green (everything's OK); yellow (I've got some concerns, but nothing desperate); and red (I'm upset). If more-specific applications of the method are needed, the temperature check can be taken at ten-minute intervals or after significant stages are reached. You can also call for more-detailed descriptions of how the person is feeling.

With these three modes of assistance in place, videoconferences can be made bearable. They are still stressful for the unconscious mind, however, and as such, they should be strictly timed, with appropriate breaks every ten minutes or so, so that participants have time to recover.

Collaboration remains the most important and most difficult aspect of virtual communication

Some business trends represent positive efforts to improve individual productivity and broader teamwork. Other trends have caused some unintended consequences of social and technological change. But all these trends have led us to our fractured, flattened, knowledge-based virtual world that leaves us overstressed, isolated, and not truly present. Supply-chain improvements led to just-in-time production and delivery—and around-the-clock work. Taking out layers of bureaucracy led to pushing authority down in the organization—and increased isolation. More-flexible working conditions led to a blurring of work and home lives. The iPhone and its relatives made all sorts of remote working possible—and meant we could always be reached. And so on down the line.

The part that none of the modern world's inventors saw coming was that this whole new host of tools would overstress the unconscious working of our brains because of what those tools provided and what they left out. The videoconference is a prime example. It enables you to be present—and yet not present. It enables you to leap over geographical distances—yet leaves you feeling more isolated than ever. It enables you to examine conditions, objects, and employees in distant places— and yet you often mistake what you see and misunderstand what you don't see.

The videoconference is an imperfect tool. You should never think of it as an adequate substitute for presence.

To improve videoconferences, work on your own personal skills

In addition to structural ways to make videoconferencing more effective, you can transform your own habits to combat the challenges of virtual interaction. Consider the following four ways to make a videoconference better.

First, change how you think. Begin by imitating the movie business; after all, you're on screen. The movie world is used to, and expert at, gathering a team for a limited time to get a job done. The people on the team may or may not know each other, but they have clearly defined roles and follow clear protocols and customs designed to control their interactions. They work together for the time it takes to make the movie, and then the team disbands.

The future of the work world will come to more closely imitate this arrangement. Consequently, clearly defining the roles for everyone at the beginning of the project, or even the single videoconference, will increase efficiency and productivity and decrease stress.

If the videoconference is part of an ongoing work stream, set up a separate database to handle all the aspects of meeting and handling the team, from calendars to to-do lists to the rules of the road and the mission, values, and goals of the project.

But remember to check on your impressions verbally during the conference; don't assume that silence implies agreement. For many occasional users of video, the experience is unsettling enough that it may inhibit their usual tendencies to voice disagreements, volunteer for further work, or otherwise participate. Regularly stop to check in, ascertain agreement or its opposite, and allow for commentary on the proceedings thus far.

You've probably got a team based all over the world; that's why you're using video. So, be sensitive to time differences, cultural differences, and levels of commitment. Human energy levels vary enormously depending on the time of day, and cultural commitments to calendars, times, and work levels vary as well. Don't assume everyone is on your clock and thinks like you.

Share documents well in advance of the meeting so that they can be downloaded and reviewed during the meeting. It's simply rude to distribute a lengthy document to all participants a few minutes before the meeting starts. Yet it happens all the time. Resist the temptation to do things at the last minute.

Speaking of advance work, have a side communications channel *and* a plan B. Technology will inevitably fail to work, so be ready. Have a secondary communications channel ready, for commenting on the main channel, and have a plan B ready in case of catastrophic failure. Circulate information about the team in advance—include both work qualifications and social tidbits. The former establishes credibility and the latter creates a more congenial atmosphere.

Further, you should establish the desired outcomes of the meeting in advance. It's important for everyone to know what they're supposed to be helping to accomplish, and having this knowledge ahead of time lowers stress.

Then, on the call, as in conference calls and webinars, practice active listening—summarizing and repeating what others say so that they feel heard. Verbally summarizing a participant's comments should primarily be the MC's or chair's responsibility, but all the participants can partake as well. And give regular feedback. Regular, timely feedback will help with team esprit de corps, individual stress, and the productivity of the meeting.

If you're dealing with multiple languages, avoid colloquialisms, and speak slower. Allow for cultural differences as well by rotating the hosting and MC-ing responsibilities, including summaries and emotional feedback. And find ways to strengthen social ties. Rotate who begins the meeting; different participants could begin different meetings by briefly talking about their home culture. Convene group activities for entertainment and fun.

Remember, like TV, the camera craves emotion. Consistent with authentic behavior, work to exaggerate and make more obvious your emotional reactions to the discussion at hand. The videoconference is not a format that likes understatement and restraint very much. Feed it what it wants. In the same vein, keep ideas, conversations, debates, and discussions as simple as possible, but no simpler. People resent having things dumbed down for them, because it feels like an implicit judgment of their worth to you, but they do appreciate simplicity when it is possible.

Second, change how you behave. Act like a TV news anchorperson. Look at the camera, smile, and project your personality. Don't watch the little picture-in-a-picture that is you. You will appear to the other person as if you are not involved, are lacking courage, are acting submissive, or all three. Don't do it! You might stand up, if the setup allows. You will project more authority and energy, and your voice will be stronger if you stand rather than sit.

Always light your surroundings brighter than seems necessary. Cameras require more light than human eyes to make a scene look naturally lit. You need to invest in good lighting in your space, or you'll look like you're talking from the dark side of the moon.

And rehearse everything. Videoconferencing is harder than it looks. Rehearse what you're going to say, rehearse how you're going to say it, and rehearse the technology. Try it out the day before you're going to connect, and the hour before.

To get all this done, you'll need help. Get both procedural help (e.g., for taking notes) and technical help (for fixing things that break). Enlisting helpers may seem like the coward's way out, but it isn't. You will appreciate the help when the inevitable happens and something does go wrong.

On the call, provide frequent callbacks and looks ahead. One of the ways you can help all the participants reduce the stress of a videoconference is by reminding people of what they've just said and foreshadowing what will come. It will help keep everyone engaged.

And just as in audioconferences and webinars, always show up early. You need time to check all the technology and get yourself focused on the task ahead.

Aim the camera down, not up. You should arrange the camera to be above your face, looking down. If you go the other way, the angle can be very unflattering to your face, and you will worry about that rather than paying attention to what's being said. The same goes for lighting—as I indicated above, you need lots of it.

For real sophistication—and kindness to your audience—arrange and layer your background like a movie set. What image do you wish to convey for yourself and your organization? The background "set" for your conference will go a long way toward showing the participants what your values, beliefs, and conditions are. Dress it up to look like the image you wish to convey. Also, create three layers of distance with simple props—near, mid-distance, and far—to create a sense of depth. This trick will lower tension with your fellow participants because it will make you look closer to the screen and reduce the need for them to shout.

Know that you are going to be judged more negatively than you would in person. A meta-analysis of a dozen studies of video job interviews found that people are less favorably regarded over video (and therefore less likely to be hired).[4] If there are important business consequences to the meeting, then think about having the meeting in person as a first option. If you are unable to do so, then think about how you can improve the outcome of the meeting in other ways.

Third, change what you do. Fundamentally, this recommendation means don't forget to move. You should close in on your own face (while looking at the camera) and use it as you would use your hands to gesture and emphasize key points, provide emotions, and help with clarity. If in doubt, practice by studying news anchors and then in front of a mirror. Like the recommendations for TV, don't wear loud stripes, checks, or anything else that could be distorted on TV. Solid colors and more conservative garb work better than do more outlandish costumes. In sum, dress for success. The single most important thing you do on a videoconference is show up looking like a pro. Too many people just dress in the costume of their tribe—business casual, suit and tie, power suit, or whatever. What can you wear that isn't freakish but that sets you apart?

Do you have any nervous tics, verbal or otherwise? If so, it's time to lose them. The first things to watch your video technique for are the obvious problems and visual idiosyncrasies that could cause the person or people on the other end of the camera to judge you negatively. And those tics will show up more prominently on video to the other person's brain because of the impoverishment of other information.

Do you have an immobile face, thanks to adrenaline? Video yourself, and study the results to see if you lose affect under stress (most of us do). If so, compensate by smiling, nodding, and opening your eyes regularly, but not all at once. Are you squinting because of the bright lights so that you look like you're confronting an unpleasant smell, not an audience of people to wow? It may be a little painful, but keep your eyes open. Otherwise, you will look suspicious or as if you hold your audience in contempt.

Are you telling a coherent story? With all the stresses of a videoconference, don't forget to practice what you're going to say and check it for coherence, interest, and common sense. Then ask, are you emotionally consistent with your message? Or are you thinking several steps ahead, already having moved on in your mind to the next part of the talk? Such a disconnected approach feels emotionally incoherent for the people on the other end of the videoconference. It's extremely difficult for an audience to understand a story that doesn't have a clear emotional line that is consistent with the meaning of the story—and one that the speaker connects with, so that the audience can, too.

In the end, the most important question is, Do you connect with the audience? One interesting thing that video tests is how strong your connection is with the other people on your videoconference. Are you truly having a conversation, or do you engage in monologues? Give your audience time to respond, show that you have listened, and regularly invite participation. And give your audience time to absorb it. Don't race to get things done. Let the others catch up, especially if the language of the meeting is not their primary one.

Be fully present with the people in the conference. That's what it all boils down to. To connect with the other participants, you need to be both emotionally present and vulnerable. With people's shorter attention spans and diminished tolerance for inauthentic behavior, you need to give others something real and to be ready to honestly share. If you phone it in, they will know. And you will know.

Sooner or later, the technology will misbehave. Be ready with your backup plans and alternative forms of communication. But also be ready to laugh; remember, it's rarely a disaster of epic proportions, and it is the human condition to fail from time to time.

Fourth, change what you say. Don't talk too much. Most speakers on conference calls, if they're not checked out, fill up the silences with their voices. They are afraid to stop, afraid to let the group go for an instant because people might stop listening, afraid to take a full emotional moment. But it's those moments that make a human connection memorable.

Talk the journey, not the destination. These days, we're so afraid of losing our participants to their short attention spans that we cut to the ending without taking our fellow combatants with us. If we're a team—or trying to become one—we have to go on the same journey.

Thus, lose the clichés and get inspired. *Don't* move the needle, drink the Kool-Aid, give due respect because it is what it is, have the necessary bandwidth, break down silos, or—God help us—experience a paradigm shift. These clichés are comforting and familiar, but they substitute for thinking. Don't utter them. Please. Do your own thinking, tell your own story, and take the team on a real journey, and you'll naturally avoid these energy killers. We get inspiration from courage, from honesty, and from triumphing over failure. No matter how many silos you break down, you can't beat honesty and courage. Inspire your fellow videoconference-goers with your real words, not borrowed ones.

Be present by listening to the others as they speak; don't plan your reply while they are speaking. There is so little real listening going on today that it is extraordinarily powerful when someone actually does us the courtesy of listening rather than thinking about what he or she is going to say. Try it.

Finally, build rapport by mirroring the other participants in your manner of speaking, your motions, and your expressions. This activity builds trust. Building (unconscious) rapport takes roughly twenty minutes at the beginning of the call. Once you've established good rapport, you can assume leadership of the meeting by proposing your desired actions and outcomes. But listen and mirror first. People want to be heard—and seen.

Videoconferencing in some ways is a richer communication experience than that infamous twentieth-century tool, the phone. But it is accordingly more stressful. The preceding ways of working on a video call can greatly improve the experience for all. Practice them, and you'll find yourself increasingly comfortable—and present—in the twenty-first century of half-real, half-virtual work and home life.

Practical fixes

The videoconference cheat sheet

Following these suggestions can vastly improve your videoconference's chances of success.

1. Imitate the movie business; after all, you're on screen.

2. If the videoconference is part of an ongoing work stream, set up a separate database to handle all the aspects of meeting and handling the team.

3. Check your impressions verbally; don't assume that silence implies agreement.

4. Be sensitive to time differences, cultural differences, and levels of commitment.

5. Share documents well in advance of the meeting so that they can be downloaded and reviewed during the meeting.

6. Have a side communications channel *and* a plan B.

7. Circulate information about the team in advance—include both work qualifications and social tidbits.

8. Establish the desired outcomes of the meeting in advance.

9. As in conference calls and webinars, practice active listening.

10. Give regular feedback.

11. If you're dealing with multiple languages, avoid colloquialisms, and speak slower.

12. Find ways to strengthen social ties.

13. Like TV, the camera craves emotion. Find ways to show your emotion.

14. Keep ideas, conversations, debates, and discussions as simple as possible, but no simpler.

15. Act like a TV news anchorperson—look at the camera, smile, and project your personality.

16. Stand up.

17. Light your surroundings brighter than seems necessary.

18. Rehearse everything.

19. Have help.

20. Provide frequent callbacks and looks ahead.

21. Just as in audioconferences and webinars, always show up early.

22. Don't forget to move.

23. Aim the camera down, not up.

24. Arrange and layer your background like a movie set.

25. Know that you are going to be judged more negatively than you would in person.

26. As recommended for TV, don't wear loud stripes, checks, or anything else that could be distorted on TV.

27. If you have any nervous tics, verbal or otherwise, try to avoid them.

28. If your face is immobile for any reason, move it!

29. If you are squinting because of the bright lights, open your eyes more.

30. Pick a coherent story, and stick to it.

31. Connect with the audience.

32. Give your audience time to absorb the messages.

33. Be fully present with the people on the conference.

34. Dress for success.

35. Sooner or later the technology will misbehave. Prepare for this eventuality.

36. Don't talk too much.

37. Talk the journey, not the destination.

38. Lose the clichés, and get inspired.

39. Be present by listening to the others as they speak; don't plan your reply while they are speaking.

40. Finally, build rapport and connection by mirroring the other participants in your manner of speaking, your motions, and your expressions.

The jump-cut story

Still worried about those incredible shrinking attention spans? Digital worlds pressure us to move quickly and capture people's attention immediately before their minds wander off again. You can grab the attention by suddenly changing the subject with a quick shift of tactics. The idea is similar to a jump cut, a film technique that abruptly shifts scenes to jar the audience. Pause for a second or two, and then begin to tell a story that ultimately has some relevance to the topic. But if the story has little immediate relevance, it will work even better—as long as it does offer an ultimate payoff. Make your listeners figure out how the story relates at first. That mental work will keep them focused.

The digital communication general cheat sheet

All the following reminders apply to any medium of virtual communication, from email to chatting to videoconferences.

1. Email, audio, video—none of it is as good as face-to-face.

2. Don't overdo—or underdo—the urgency of a communication.

3. Don't give in to the urge to short-circuit.

4. Don't automate the un-automatable.

5. Know what you're trying to achieve.

6. Make a commitment to communication.

7. Consciously agree on the forms and periodicity of communication that everyone will use.

8. Establish a virtual message hierarchy.

9. Make cultural differences a conscious part of your communication.

10. Set up several communication channels so that you can communicate quickly in case of emergency.

CHAPTER SUMMARY

- Videoconferencing is hard; take it seriously.

- It's not the same as being there; recognize the differences, and practice for success.

- Figure out a way to make turn-taking clear.

- Assign an MC.

- Add a regular, formal perception check.

10.

SALES

The internet and mobile phone together have changed our notions of friendship, family relationships, work connections, and personal ties. Whereas in the past we might have had regular, close interaction with immediate family, friends, and coworkers and weaker ties with a larger social circle we saw infrequently, we now might interact frequently with our weak-tie friends, perhaps less than with our closer connections, but perhaps more. Indeed, many people today seem to have fewer in-person relationships and more weak-tie virtual relationships.

The result for many people is greater feelings of loneliness and, for a tragic few, an increase in suicide.[1] Indeed, there's a direct correlation between the number of hours teenage girls spend on their mobile phones and their incidence of depression and suicide.[2] These consequences are not because mobile phones and weak-tie friendships are bad things, but because the human psyche is fed on in-person interaction. And at the same time, we may interact less frequently in person with our work colleagues and friends because they are spread all over the world and our ties with them are mainly virtual.

The photograph of the era is not something you see in *Life* magazine, but a selfie. My wife and I still marvel over the time a year or two ago, when we tried to get into the room where the

Mona Lisa is displayed in the Louvre, only to be turned back by the crowds. They weren't studying this great work of art; instead, they were taking selfies in the same room as the great painting. They were in the same room as a painting that the Western world generally agrees is its greatest work of art, and they were taking pictures of themselves.

The Facebook generations have turned in on themselves and become self-referential. The documentation of the event is more important that the event itself.

But self-referentialism is not the same thing as selfishness. These are not bad people. It's just that they want to be able to post the picture to Facebook or Instagram to show their family, friends, colleagues—and weak-tie acquaintances—that they were somewhere notable.

In that context, how can you sell people things, services, and ideas? Has it become harder or easier to infect people with the desire to purchase that latest gizmo, service, or idea?

The sales cycle has changed

First and most important, the internet has fundamentally changed the sales cycle. When salespeople connect with a potential customer, they typically do so much further along the sales journey. The potential customer has already researched the possible options and the ratings of your company and your rivals.

For this reason, salespeople need to learn new techniques of selling—establishing a personal connection quickly, checking in on the stage of the sales journey appropriately, and moving the customer along at the right pace. All this relationship management must be conducted half in the real world and half in the virtual world. Because the exact balance will depend on the customer or client, the salesperson not only needs to have facility in both worlds but also needs the ability to read the customer quickly and ascertain how to best connect with the person or group in the sales cycle. These requirements make listening, something that has always been important, especially important in the virtual-real world.

Your customer's needs take priority, even over your product

Most salespeople know that they should listen to the client, but too few of them do, and usually not soon enough. And they don't listen in the right way. You should be listening for the under-lying messages more than the superficial ones. What emotion is the (potential) customer putting forward? Excitement about a new purchase? Fear about a new technology? Resistance to change? Resentment toward the old product?

What's memorable—and important to people—in com-munication is emotion; that's what you should be listening for and responding to, not just the expressed content. If you acknowledge a client's emotions and figure out an appropriate way to respond to them, you'll be the favorite salesperson in no time.

Begin by establishing a connection. That means understand-ing where your customers and clients live in the universe of weak-tie relationships. You need to be in the same networks.

We want to feel that connection is real and strong enough to last through the after-sale (or repeat-sale) care, so don't rush it or fake it. Connections between people get established at the surface first, but if they're to be durable, then they must have emotional glue to hold them together.

In the virtual world, what other people say is more important than what you say

Because we don't know whom to trust online and our online trust relationships are more fragile than they are in person, we look to third-party endorsements to help us believe that a salesperson, whether of purses or cars, is on the up-and-up. Successful salespeople will invest heavily in online networks to begin to generate these third-connections and endorsements. They are the sales lifeblood of your new persona in the current sales world and in the future.

You find the endorsements and then sit back and let the customers find you. Well, of course it's not that simple, and you need to market and advertise harder than ever in the channels your customers frequent. But customers now own the sales cycle to a much greater extent. It is your job to wait until they are ready for the close—unless they signal to you that they do want help along the way.

To close a sale, you need to have established two things with your customer: credibility and trust. And it's credibility first and trust second. Credibility comes first, because that's what happens when you show that you understand the customer's problem. Trust comes second, because that's what you establish when you solve that problem.

It's all about credibility and trust

Failing either one, your relationship with the client or customer won't be durable. Without credibility, you'll find that your customers will be likely to go elsewhere in search of expertise, even if they trust you as a human being. *Do you really understand my paint color issues?* Without trust, a client will be tempted to mine you for expertise and then go make the ultimate purchase from someone else. *Will you really follow through on the after-sale?*

How do you establish these two key aspects of a relationship? By listening. Show that you understand the issues as well as, or better than, the client does, and you'll create credibility. *She gets that I loathe chartreuse! Finally, someone who knows something about paint!*

Then, show how you can solve that problem. You'll forge a strong bond of trust with the client when you take away the point of pain that sent the client to the marketplace in the first place. *That shade of lavender will be perfect for the room.*

Credibility and trust underlie online sales success. They are the two key ingredients for building a strong, enduring relationship with a customer. Closing a sale is all about understanding the customer's half-online, half-real decision-making process.

Where are your clients or customers when they get in touch with you?

Are they happy with the product they have, but want to be reassured that they made the right decision? Put them in the database to check in with them periodically so that you'll have a relationship established when they are ready to change.

Customers in the first stages of decision making just need help with framing the problem. Less information is better. Just give them a statistic or a very brief verbal portrait of what the future might look like. *Do you realize that the 2019 version of the Fabulator uses half the energy of its predecessors?*

Or are they in the throes of the problem, uncertain of which way to go, looking for answers? Jump in with helpful links, information, and unbiased advice. This is the point to become as un-sales-y as it is possible to get. Customers deep in the problem want information—comparisons, data, details. At this stage, all the product or service knowledge you have is actually useful. Don't go to the point of their eyes glazing over, but do satisfy their urge for information. *Both models will get the job done, but the Fabulator-B is smaller and quieter, not to mention faster-operating.*

Or have they already decided on a course of action and are basically looking for you to take the order? More and more customers are coming to salespeople in that state of mind. It's just a matter of recognizing this stage of readiness and negotiating the deal. Clients who have already made up their mind don't want to be slowed down, so don't make it hard for them to buy. *You've made a great choice. The Fabulator Supreme will take care of all your needs and also make you a spectacular cup of morning coffee. Now let's get that paperwork out of the way.*

That's why it's so important to listen to your customers before you launch into any kind of explanation. If you don't know where they are, you can't point them to where they should be going.

Finally, involve your customers with small steps to get them comfortable to take the bigger ones. It's imperative that you don't do all the work in the sales process. If you keep your customers passive, don't be surprised when it's hard for them to suddenly get active and agree to close the sale. Too many salespeople think that it's all up to them. But the real secret is to get the customer working on the deal, too. Begin with little steps, those that don't involve big commitments, and then work up from there.

Don't throw dollar bills on the floor

In the 1987 comedy *Tin Men*, 1960s-era aluminum siding salesman Bill "BB" Babowsky, played by Richard Dreyfuss, initiates a younger protégé into the magical world of sales.[3] In one call on a homemaker, Babowsky drops a dollar bill on the floor and allows the woman to pick it up for him. He explains to the initiate that he can tell whether or not he's going to get a sale with this trick. If the woman picks up the bill, she's a nice person and can be talked into aluminum siding. If she doesn't, she won't be won over.

The psychology is right, but the execution is wrong. Babowsky should have been seeking to create a real trust relationship with his customers, or his partner, rather than just exploiting them. And by getting them involved, not in sneaky tests of their malleability, but in genuine steps along the road to the sale, he would have increased the amount of aluminum siding gracing the houses of Baltimore.

Take your customers from passive to active. Involve them in the process. Don't do all the work. If you take your customers on the right journey, you will move them smoothly and comfortably from connection to trust to commitment to sale.

And don't forget to let other people speak for you. That's the essence of sales success in the virtual world. But you also need to become comfortable with, and expert in, the networked world. More and more people spend more and more time on mobile phones in the Facebook, Instagram, and Snapchat universe. They access these worlds constantly throughout the workday and on their own time as well. These worlds essentially run 24-7, and you need to be responsive. You need to understand how your particular customer set lives in the real-virtual collision of worlds and how they want to be messaged, connected with, and sold to.

How can you create reciprocity?

In the online world, then, once you've established a connection, think about creating reciprocity. What can you do that will create people's sense of obligation to you? Not so huge that it induces guilt, but enough so that the person wants to do something for you.

The next step online is to get permission and establish the right levels of interactivity. Don't get pushy; do get permission to use their name, to email them, to call them—whatever the relationship might consist of—respecting their need not to be hounded or outed.

Then, think about how much interaction they are ready for. It's easy online to overdo it, because interaction is relatively friction-free. It doesn't cost much, so you tend to err on the side of too much rather than too little. Get the amounts right.

Do so by asking; don't try to guess. Online, it's best to be formal about the privacy, handshake, interaction, and other relationship rules first and then to be informal about the relationship itself. Share your sources and links, and be open about what you're up to. The potential customer or client is going to find out anyway, and information on you is only a few clicks and minutes away. Online or in person, don't try to be something you're not.

Fundamentally, it's good to remember that the brain's basic responses haven't changed online. To connect with people, get their attention first. Then engage their emotions and activate their memories. Use novelty to surprise them and get them moving toward a sale. When they're ready, or close to it, motivate interest with the classic methods of influence: authority, liking, scarcity, commitment, consistency, social proof, and reciprocity.

Use people to connect to people

We humans are most interested in other humans—what their intent is; what they look like; and what they might do to us, for us, or with us. We like to engage with other people, internet kittens and puppies notwithstanding. We seek ways to alleviate pain, we are drawn to contrast, and we like to be rewarded for our efforts. We're biased toward attractive people, baby faces, and aesthetically pleasing objects. We're fascinated by archetypes and anthropomorphic forms. We find pictures of nature relaxing and cities stimulating. And always, the simpler the better.

When we're wearing our logical hats, we believe that hard work is always rewarded; that feedback improves us; that if we do a good job, politics doesn't matter; that our work speaks for itself; and that persuasiveness is logic and facts. None of those statements is actually true.

Emotionally, we want to be understood, heard, and valued. We want to be treated as a respected member of the team. Yet we want autonomy, too. Our status must be acknowledged, and our role understood. None of those desires is logical, but they are extremely important to relationships, and thus sales.

There are many kinds of roles and relationships that you can use to successfully influence a sales process: mentor, partner, storyteller, learner, backup, celebrity, decision maker, provider, guide, performer, supporter, ambassador, and so forth. To be successful in the long run, pick one of these roles, and become expert in it. They are recognizable and understood, and the clarity helps online.

Memory can be a challenge in the virtual world

The statistics of remembering are unkind to salespeople everywhere. The research shows that people don't remember much overall, they don't remember the details well, and they especially don't retain stuff that they disagree with or that conflicts with their worldview.[4] Apparently, when we don't like what we hear, we just tune it out.

Into this depressing landscape comes a spate of recent studies finding simple ways to improve memory and retention.[5] If you are a salesperson, you can use these ideas to ensure that your customers remember something of what you worked so hard to get those fickle people to pay attention to.

First, an overall strategy. Again, you need to make the customers do some of the work. That way, they will feel that they own, at least in part, the result. So, get them telling stories, designing solutions, playing games, competing for recognition, brainstorming, making real choices, or teaching. When customers help cocreate the relationship, they feel deeply involved and they remember far more of what has gone on.

What else can you do? Have your clients use their imagination rather than their intellect—especially how it relates to them. Using our imagination invokes the emotions, and the emotional part of our minds is where decisions are made. Get your clients or customers involved for forty seconds or more. This length of time seems to strengthen memory. So does writing something down, as opposed to speaking or typing something. The physical act of writing is a powerful aid to memory. Drawing pictures helps anchor the memory, too.

Mirroring is also a key to memory

Finally, we are more inclined to trust people who look and feel similar to us, and you are precisely raising that trust when you mirror someone. Recent studies show that mirroring makes a sales pitch 20 percent more effective, and that in salary negotiations, you can get up to one-third more money by mirroring your potential boss during the bargaining.[6] You don't have to be face-to-face to mirror, because you can use the patterns of the voice on a phone call or even repeat patterns of word usage in an email, but of course, mirroring works much more powerfully face-to-face.

Humans—and indeed primates in general—copy one another unconsciously when they agree with one another, feel comfortable with others, or want to show solidarity with them. Most of us are usually completely unaware of this behavior at the conscious level. If things are going well for you in a conversation, and you can spare some of your precious conscious thought for noticing it, you'll see the other person or people mirroring you to the extent that they can, depending on how they are situated in relation to you.

When you become aware of mirroring behavior, you'll see it everywhere. You'll begin to understand how the best salespeople persuade customers so effortlessly, how the most successful politicians bind voters to them despite the issues, and how the most powerful executives build trust among their direct reports and colleagues.

Mirroring reflects alignment. When we're aligned with someone, we mirror the person's behavior, and vice versa. When you meet someone for the first time, if you like and begin to trust him or her, you'll demonstrate that affinity with mirroring. You may demonstrate it in other ways as well, but mirroring is probably the most reliable indicator of the growing bond between you.

This sort of mirroring will seem utterly obvious to you, but if you perform it smoothly and subtly, without overdoing it or responding too quickly or mechanically, the other person or people will never notice consciously what you're doing. You will make a much stronger connection with them and make them feel much more positively and trusting toward you. Don't neglect this simple body-language tool in your sales toolbox.

Meet a successful virtual salesperson

Ryan Estis started out as a traditional, pound-the-pavement salesman, making cold calls and driving all over town to get a few minutes of face time with a potential customer. He didn't set out to do so much of his work online. But he has become incredibly successful at selling in the virtual space. He is in high demand as a keynote speaker, and he and his team are constantly busy fielding calls from new clients.[7]

"I still believe there's no replacement for face-to-face interaction," Estis says. But a world where face-to-face interaction often comes after weeks or months of virtual interaction online creates new challenges for salespeople—and new opportunities.

The digital world we all inhabit today is fast-paced and flooded with information. "Customers today are time-poor," Estis says. "They're distracted, they're overwhelmed, they have shorter attention spans, there's more noise out there." Breaking through that noise can be an enormous challenge. And yet, Estis says, "I believe that the opportunity far outweighs the challenge."

The world is more connected than ever—a situation that creates huge opportunities for connecting with customers. "This is the single greatest time to be in the profession of business development in the history of the world," Estis says, "because the world is a connected place."

Sales used to be all about relationships, Estis says. Today, it still is—but those relationships can be formed and sustained in new and different ways. "Selling today is no longer about who you know," Estis says. "It's about who knows you. It's about getting referred and getting found." Estis says he no longer makes cold calls. He makes "warm calls," reaching out to people who already know of him, either because of his reputation or because they've been referred by a satisfied customer.

Become a subject-matter expert

So how do you get found? How do you set yourself up to make these warm calls? The first step is to set yourself up as an expert in your field. No matter what business you're in, you're facing more competition than ever before, Estis says. "Customers are overwhelmed. They have the paradox of choice," he says.

Imagine, for example, that you want to book a vacation. What would you do first? Go online and start looking at options—and within five minutes, you'll have more options than you could ever possibly evaluate. You'll be looking next for expert advice to help you sort through this flood of information.

Blogging is one great way to set yourself up as an expert. Rumors of the death of blogging are greatly exaggerated. It may change—and it is changing—from the traditional written post, to visual, video, and pictorial versions. And, of course, there are other ways to create content that positions you as a reliable source of information. But the key is consistency, Estis says. Don't try it for a month or two and then conclude it's a waste of time. Estis has been blogging regularly for eight years. "Writing and publishing three times a week is hard, but it makes sales easier," he says. "By being known as a more credible expert, it makes me a more credible salesperson."

Referrals have always been one of the best ways to drive sales, but they're more important than ever in a world where customers are drowning in information. "It's amazing how many salespeople don't simply ask for referrals," Estis says, "and put themselves in a position to earn referrals." This old-world skill is crucial in the new digital world.

The first step is to exceed your customer's expectations, Estis says: "Earn the right to ask, then ask." And once you've asked, make it easy for people to refer you. Make yourself easy to find online, so that a customer can share your website, your Twitter handle, or a piece of content you've created. Ultimately, Estis says, "we want to turn our customers into evangelists." Make it so your customers can't help but spread the word about you. A must-share online presence is hard to create, but it makes sales easy, Estis says.

The cold call might as well be dead

The cold call may not exactly be dead, but it's certainly not your best option in a world where customers have so many demands on their time. "It's always better to be found than to have to be the one initiating contact," Estis says. But "if you're going to initiate contact, the more customized and personal it can be, the better."

Keep in mind that your call is interrupting your potential client's day. "You've got to earn the right to interrupt somebody," Estis says. And that means doing as much preparation as you can before you pick up the phone.

Customization and personalization are critical in today's information-rich world. "The traditional approaches to selling still have merit," Estis says, "but you just have to think about them differently." It has always been a good idea to customize your pitch for each customer, but today you have a lot of new tools available. If you've got a call scheduled with a potential client, you can look the person up on LinkedIn, Twitter, Instagram, and other social media sites.

Estis and his team research their prospects before they speak and send over content that's relevant to their particular problems before a call. "It just changes the conversation," he says. "The sale is closed. All they have to do is hear my voice and know I'm still breathing."

Creating a sense of urgency can also help move potential clients to a decision point. With so much information at our fingertips, Estis notes, it's easy to put off making a purchase. "The sales cycle is lengthening, because people are overwhelmed. They have the paradox of choice," he says. "I've been shopping for a new car for seven years." Of course, this sense of urgency has to be genuine. Customers will quickly be turned off by an inauthentic, used-car-salesperson kind of vibe.

"Professional selling should be about helping people solve a problem or accelerate an opportunity," Estis says. If you genuinely believe your product is the customer's best solution, that belief will come through. And if you can come up with a genuine reason why acting now is in the customer's best interest, you'll be able to cut through all the noise and make the sale.

Technology has changed the way we live and work enormously, and it just keeps changing. The best way to approach this era of rapid change is to think of yourself as a student, Estis says. "The best salespeople today are students, and they're teachers," he says. That means keeping up with new technological tools, and trying them out. Should you be on Snapchat? How could you use Instagram Stories for your business?

"The best performers are constantly striving to level up their game," Estis says. You should always be experimenting with new tools and techniques, and always be refining your approach.

Of course, the more independent you are, the easier it is to try out new tools and experiment with your approach to sales. But whether you're an entrepreneur or a salesperson within a corporation, you should use whatever tools are available to you, Estis says.

If you work for a big company, familiarize yourself with all the marketing tools at your disposal, and try out different ways of using them with clients. Try publishing your ideas on LinkedIn or whatever social media you can use. And keep in mind that "it's not just what you're sharing; it's what you're learning," Estis says. Even if you're limited in your ability to blog or get your name out there, you can connect with potential customers online and get a better sense of who they are and what drives them. That's an old-fashioned value—knowing your customer—brought into the new digital world.

Practical fixes

The ten commandments of online sales and sales presentations

I. Thou shalt speak and write authentically, avoiding all marketing BS and self-serving promotion. Thou shalt sound as *little* like an American presidential candidate as possible, not trying to promise all things to all people.

II. Thou shalt focus on the other person. The success of a communication ultimately belongs to the receiver, not to the speaker. Thou shalt realize that in the end, it is the client that is important, not thee.

III. Thou shalt not use PowerPoint to present sales pitches. Nay, nor Keynote, nor Prezi, nor any other slide software, as glitzy as it might be.

IV. Thou shalt not begin thy pitch with a joke.* Thou shalt remember that humor is personal, local, and as likely to offend as it is to please. Especially political humor. Thou shalt derive thy humor spontaneously from the situation and the customer in front of thee, not from one-liners. (*Unless thou art really, really funny.)

V. Thou shalt speak with all appropriate passion and not be boring. Thou shalt refrain from the dreaded information dump. Thou shalt help the customer by sharing the high points of thy wisdom, not the entire body of knowledge thou hast.

VI. Thou shalt tell stories and not kill thy customer with endless data. Thou shalt tell stories with a minimum of detail and a maximum of drama. Thou shalt tell real stories and refrain from retailing anecdotes with little point and no excitement.

VII. Thou shalt not make a sales pitch for thy company or thy services before the customer has indicated readiness. Thou shalt not sell without being asked in any shape, form, or way. Thou shalt be content with implicit selling of the sort that comes from doing a good job.

VIII. Thou shalt not begin with talk of thyself. Nor shalt thou begin with an agenda or an agenda slide. Nor shalt thou begin with aimless chitchat about the color of thy tie or thy relationship to thine organization.

IX. Thou shalt not speak through thy nose or at the floor. If thou dost insist on using slides, thou shalt not speak while regarding them with admiration. Thou shalt not argue with thy slides. Thou shalt not need to interpret the thousand numbers on thy slides, because thou shalt not have a thousand numbers on thy slides.

X. Thou shalt not exceed thine allotted time. Thou shalt not answer thine own questions. Thou shalt not find the sound of thine own voice more fascinating than anyone else's, especially the customer's.

The online sales cheat sheet

All the ideas this book has proposed for virtual communication also apply to the salesperson-customer relationship. But the following suggestions can help you fine-tune your online sales skills.

1. Begin by listening to discover the customer's state of need. Don't sell yourself; get third-party endorsements to do the work.

2. Referrals are more important than ever.

3. Establish credibility by offering the right information depending on where the customer is in the sales-decision journey.

4. Establish trust by solving the customer's problem.

5. Look to establish a relationship that lasts beyond the sale.

6. Involve the customer in the process; don't do all the work for the customer.

7. Mirror your customer's language, habits, and practices—but keep it real.

8. Become a subject-matter expert in your field.

9. Customization and personalization are more important than ever.

CHAPTER SUMMARY

- The internet has profoundly changed the sales cycle.

- You can use the weak-tie relationships of the online world to establish credibility.

- It's best to seek third-party endorsements rather than trumpet your own success.

- Customers manage their own sales decisions and typically come to you much further along in the cycle.

- Listening is therefore more important than ever.

- Online, pay attention to how your customers remember—and how they forget.

- Become a trusted source of information—a subject-matter expert—in your field.

CONCLUSION

Something basic is changing about the way we form relationships in the digital world. Will the next generations be able to invest in online connections the same way that everyone now invests in "real" face-to-face relationships?

As I've mentioned, the nature of trust in the virtual world has changed forever. Trust is much more fragile, though perhaps easier to establish initially. But the big difference comes when something threatens the trust. In face-to-face relationships where there is trust, one party may do something to screw up, causing friction, anger, and even a bit of mistrust to creep in. But if the connection is strong enough, the issue will get thrashed out, the perpetrator will apologize, and trust will be restored. Indeed, once restored, the trust may be stronger than ever.

How different the situation is in the virtual world! Once trust is threatened, it's instantly broken, and it's virtually impossible to reestablish it. People simply move on. Since trust was more fragile in the first place, it shatters with very little provocation.

We must face the final virtual problem

If most of your relationships are virtual, the fragility of those relationships may make you less able to get through the bumps and shocks that every (face-to-face) relationship naturally endures. If you take the pattern of commitment from the virtual world, your understanding of the meaning of relationship will be attenuated and weak.

And these weaker ties mean we inhabit a more toxic world. The research shows that negative conversations stay with us longer than do positive ones because of how we metabolize oxytocin and cortisol differently.[1] How will we evolve as we move into a more and more virtual existence? Today, we still live in both worlds—face-to-face relationships and virtual ones. But how will we act in 2050? Or 2100?

What could the future look like?

I hope we'll learn to live in a variety of worlds and become proficient in many of them, code-switching easily, with perhaps an inevitably attenuated sense of emotional participation in all of them. That's the future. Instead of having work and home and perhaps a third world of an outside interest or a pub, we'll have many worlds, half real and half virtual, some all virtual, and few all real. The adepts will be people who can move from one world to the next with ease. You will learn to switch between worlds, but will also be comfortable with inhabiting—and having everyone you know inhabiting—a variety of worlds.

As the saying goes, generals fight the last war. They use a strategy aimed at the war they've already fought. In today's business world, we're not showing ourselves to be any wiser. We still communicate in nonvirtual ways and expect those approaches to work in the virtual environment. We instead need to learn new ways of working.

We have the choice of worlds now, virtual, real, virtual-1, virtual-2, virtual-3—one at a time or all at once. We may interact with work colleagues on various text-based platforms. We may message friends and family. We may participate in online fantasy sports or other online gaming worlds. Our hobbies may have online versions or chat functions. We need to either learn to embrace more worlds at once—with less attention paid in each—or embrace one world even more deeply. Hence the popularity, after the work day is over, of watching TV while hanging out with the family and catching up on email. Or, setting everything else aside to binge-watch *Game of Thrones* for most of the weekend.

But as part of embracing more worlds or one world more deeply, we need to learn to use new criteria for what constitutes attention. We've come to expect instant responses to our virtual queries from employees, spouses, and others while at the same time deploring other people's lack of attention because they're texting while we speak to them face-to-face. These are symptoms of our halting efforts to adapt to the new virtual multiverse. We're using old criteria for what constitutes attention.

What are the new rules? How can we make them work? How can we make it worthwhile to work virtually and find it as satisfying as face-to-face work can be? In the virtual world, you have to become more intentional and clear about putting the emotions into what you're doing, rather than taking them for granted as you could in the face-to-face world. What does that look like?

In the virtual world, we have to be intentional about emotion

In the old, face-to-face world, we could afford to be lazy about our communications, relying on our unconscious minds to do most of the work. In the new world, we have to be intentional about our emotions. Now, we realize how hard it is to get it right, to deliver emotions with sensitivity, to communicate precisely what's needed. We're becoming more aware of how complicated those relations always were.

What can we do to make all our communication more successful in the virtual world? The following are my final top eight if-you-get-nothing-else-from-this-book takeaways for improving virtual communication.

Begin by accepting the less-than-perfect nature of virtual communication. Don't try to make virtual communication into something it's not or try to make it carry freight it can't. Do the less important things via virtual meetings whenever possible. Save the emotional stuff for face-to-face meetings because it's emotions and attitudes that are conveyed mostly through body language.

Schedule regular face-to-face meetings to reinvigorate the team. If you are kicking off something important, are celebrating a big win, or have significant problems to discuss, bite the meeting bullet and bring everyone together. Trying to solve disagreements or rev people up via a digital phone line is pure folly and engineered disappointment. Our emotional investment in a phone call is simply less than in a face-to-face meeting, and the lack of visual and tonal information makes it much harder to get key messages across.

Never go longer than ten minutes in any format without some kind of break. The breaks will allow people to reengage. You can either stop the meeting entirely or just urge everyone to get up and stretch. People don't need a long break, just a chance for a quick change of pace. Keep your text-based communications short, too.

Get regular group input. What most people do during long phone meetings is put the phone on mute and take care of other chores while half-listening. You can keep the group involved by going around the phones asking for input. In a face-to-face meeting, you're able to tell how people are doing by monitoring their body language. In a virtual meeting, you need to stop regularly to take everyone's temperature. And I do mean everyone. Go right around the list, asking each locale or person for input. If you're really gutsy, let people know they'll be quizzed; research suggests they'll remember more if you suggest that they'll be asked about things after the meeting.[2]

Have an MC. The group can't run itself without the virtual equivalent of body language. You need someone who's in charge of making sure that each person talks and that everyone is engaged.

Identify your emotions verbally. Lacking visual cues, we have a very hard time reading other people's feelings, so make yours clear verbally and train other people on the call to do the same. Say, "I'm excited about everything we're accomplishing!" Or, "Bob, I'm concerned that you don't seem confident in the third-quarter numbers. How are you really feeling about them?" You've got to put back in what the digital links are removing.

Use video to bring the group together. Face-to-face meetings allow a group to share emotions easily. Such sharing keeps them together and feeling connected. Sharing your emotions is much harder to do in a virtual meeting. So do the small talk—but make it video small talk. Get the group to send each other thirty-second or one-minute clips of what they're up to or what the weather's like where they are. Something personal really adds a sense of connection back to the group. Put some of that money you're saving on travel to good technological use. It's not a perfect solution, but it will help.

Finally, embrace the technology; don't fight it. And don't fight the last war. The virtual world we have created is not going away. We need to learn new ways to cope and behave in the virtual space. Just as we have to learn how to be savvy citizens of the "real" business world, now we need to learn the rules and tricks of the virtual business world.

How will our new digital worlds change us?

People are going to google you. They're googling you now, in fact. To have a conversation in the future, we will call up holograms of each other, with all the essential facts about each of us hovering in space above the person. You can't hide yourself in the virtual world. But you can shape yourself.

Take charge of your persona before it takes charge of you

If your online presence and your current content—what you're selling, talking about, or arguing for—don't align, the people are going to believe the online persona that's already out there. On August 3, 2017, a judge in Massachusetts sentenced Michelle Carter, who was twenty, to fifteen months in prison for exhorting her boyfriend to kill himself via text message. Her online persona, in the form of those saved text messages, had preceded her and left her (and her lawyer's) arguments in the dust of credibility.[3] In that case, her online world (with her boyfriend) and her real world collided, and prison time was the result.

In the classic 1950s mentality, home and work were two very separate spheres with very little overlap. Now we're increasingly living in all our worlds at once—even if they don't collide with fatal consequences. You're at work, texting your friends about your fantasy football league, looking at pictures from your trip to Comic-Con, where you ran into your boss dressed as a stormtrooper. All these worlds are half physical and half virtual, and increasingly, they all connect with one another. The true adepts in these worlds of the future will be people who develop the ability to code-switch from one world to the next—while maintaining a consistent and authentic personality that works seamlessly in all the worlds.

But that's only the beginning. Research shows that millennials demand greater and greater transparency from their leaders.[4] When their managers say jump, they don't say, "How high?" They say, "Why?" or "What will this accomplish?" or "How high will you be jumping?" This demand for transparency is increasingly the new reality in the world of work, and it has huge implications for everyone. Not only must team leaders and managers work much harder to show their teams how their work contributes to the broader mission, but team members must also be prepared to work more collaboratively and with more eyes on their progress than ever before. The rise of digital communications has inverted power relationships, empowered customers, and changed the nature of the employer-employee relationship forever.

Let's close this book about the perils of virtual communications by looking at a couple of trends. One that might be considered right at the epicenter of the real-versus-virtual collision is virtual reality, or VR.

Virtual reality eventually replaces most face-to-face meetings

Kristopher Blom has been working in virtual reality since 1998.[5] At the time, movies and books had made many promises about what VR would be like, but the technology was still far from ready for the mainstream. "At the time, VR was extremely expensive," Blom says. The devices involved looked nothing like the simple head-mounted displays you see today. These early VR systems would project images into an entire room. "There weren't a lot of people who got to use them," Blom says.

But even at this early stage in the development of VR, the technology could start creating the sense that two people in different places were sharing the same virtual space. The first question, Blom says, was, "Can we have a shared experience where we're both virtually in the same space?" In those early days, researchers could create a shared virtual space, but "there wasn't much of a representation of me or you on the other end," he says. You might have an avatar that represented you in the space, but it couldn't do much to reflect your movements.

Today, of course, the technology has improved greatly, but the goals are still largely the same: create a shared virtual experience for people who aren't physically in the same place. Blom has worked on research that involves creating an avatar to represent a user's body, so that when you look down, you see a body that's moving in the same ways you do. "This experience is very powerful," Blom says. "Our brains are so plastic that we can accept that that body is ours nearly instantaneously."

Blom now works on a product called the Virtual Orator, which aims to help people conquer their fear of public speaking by allowing them to practice on a virtual audience. "It's kind of the tool I wish I'd had, so that I didn't have to learn public speaking the hard way," he says.

The virtual audience can be programmed to respond positively or negatively. Either way, the key is how much the virtual experience feels like the real experience of speaking in front of an audience. "You have to practice looking at the people, and you don't practice in the same way as you would normally," Blom says. "Once you really get into practicing, they become people."

The VR experience is so powerful, Blom explains, because "we're visual people." Our visual sense tends to dominate our other senses. "As long as what we give you is visual input, basically the brain has very little choice but to accept this as reality."

That's bad news for many of the ways we communicate in the virtual space today. It's one of the reasons conference calls are so difficult, for example. But VR is getting closer and closer to replicating the experience of being in the same room, Blom says. Certain things can help immensely. "If we've all been to the same space—for instance, corporate headquarters—when we have a virtual experience that's in the same space, that really grounds that experience," he says.

Researchers today are working on technologies that allow for better and better avatars in virtual environments, Blom says. Right now, an avatar can replicate broad movements like the way your arms and legs are moving and can show which direction you're looking in. But startups are currently working on software that can create a digital version of your face from photographs or match smaller facial movements. "These kinds of things are going to happen more and more," Blom says. Not too long from now, he says, "we can have a virtual-face-to-virtual-face where that face is actually us."

It will take a while before technology can replicate things like microexpressions, which make face-to-face communication so rich, Blom says. But in the meantime, our experiences in VR can do a lot to enrich our understanding of how we communicate.

Holograms replace travel

As we learn to embrace VR and other such advanced means of communication, we'll get more and more comfortable with our virtual selves projected in physical space. The next frontier of not being present is being present in a virtual sense.

All the trends toward less permanent work arrangements, in terms of both employment and office space, will add momentum to this idea of the avatar as an actual replacement for our physical bodies. Both cost and convenience align here, and the trend will be hard to stop.

The office as a traditional place for groups of people to meet, sit, and do coordinated work projects will become obsolete. IBM has reduced the office space it occupies by seventy-eight million square feet in the last two decades, saving $100 million annually.[6] That's just one company in one twenty-year period. Future generations won't know what the word *office* means. They'll still work, but not in that space.

Face-to-face conferences will still happen for special occasions

We humans can't rewire quickly enough to do away with face-to-face conferences for now. Indeed, we'll have in-person conferences for the next century at least. Why? There are a few reasons. Conferences offer work teams and individuals a change of perspective. They are a good way to get out of your rut.

Most importantly, conferences offer organizations and their employees the opportunity for powerful face-to-face encounters. Because of the way our brains are constructed, with mirror neurons that fire with the emotions of the people around us, face-to-face meetings provide important experiences that we can't get virtually—at least not for a long time to come.

Moreover, conferences offer people a chance to focus in an information-saturated world. It's difficult for us humans to focus online because of the lack of emotional reward in the impoverished channels we use. At the same time, we get quick little boosts of endorphins from checking email, glancing at Facebook, checking Instagram, and so forth, because the constant updates associated with these online worlds are like little sugar rushes for us. Consequently, we're constantly distracted and need face-to-face breaks from online distraction for deeper human meaning to be exchanged. And busy, stressed-out employees need a chance to think about the office away from the office—for as long as we still have offices.

Virtual meetings can work well where there is already a relationship established, but they are very poor ways to initiate human relationships. Certain reactions only happen between people in close proximity. As you know by now, perhaps the most important of these is trust. Online trust is fragile, shallow, and, once broken, impossible to restore.

Virtual isolation will continue to add to our social anxiety

We'll continue to get in touch with more and more people, but it will be the virtual version of these people, and not the real one, that we connect with all too often. These virtual connections will leave the unconscious mind unsatisfied.

We have all this fear, thanks to the pace of change and the randomness of the future, that the future will be something awful. But logic dictates that a surprising amount of our future will be a repeat of something we've done in the past. We think the same thoughts, go to the same places, and argue with the same people—over and over again. A good deal of our angst, therefore, inevitably comes from replaying the recent past, wishing it had gone better, and wondering what we might have done differently.

Sages have long counseled us to let go of the past because we can't change it. But I don't think their counsel really gets at the heart of the problem. We obsess about the past because we fear replaying the same patterns tomorrow, or the next day. We look backward, negotiating with our memories, trying to make them come out differently to control the future.

But of course we can't control the future. Instead, we need to look forward, thinking to ourselves, "What's one small thing I can change to affect the outcome when that scenario comes around again?" Otherwise, it's *Groundhog Day* for everyone, and who wants that?

If you're clear about why you're moving forward, whom you're moving forward with, and how moving forward might be only slightly different—you just might pull it off. And your future then can be a wholly positive one.

It doesn't have to be this way

Finally, what might the virtual world look like in the future if it really worked well? How might it help us have more satisfying, fulfilled lives rather than—as it does now—promoting hate, creating envy, and inducing us all to believe that somewhere, somehow, someone else is having a better time than we are?

I see five desiderata that the online world could aspire to offer to make the world a better place for humans.

First, the online world would focus more on the future than on the past. Currently, we google random things to settle bets with our spouses about that bit of movie trivia, or to catch up on the news, or to see what we've missed on Facebook. The internet shows us what we already know. How could it bring us more possibilities and suggestions, rather than the present sorry state of things and the past?

In the movies, the purpose of augmented reality is to complement the abilities of the wearer of some cool device. Our current internet just tells us what we already know. It intensifies our tendencies rather than pointing us in interesting new directions.

Second, the online world would become more crowdsourced and user generated. The current trend on the internet is for the huge dominant players like Facebook to become increasingly powerful and to choose what we see more and more thoroughly. Already, my feed has become a mix of advertisements for products related to something that I just googled. *Thinking about a trip to Italy? Here's some premium luggage!* This trend needs to be reversed, and we need more people sharing real wisdom with the world.

Third, the internet should help us create, weave, and tell better stories about our lives. Even Facebook does a miserable job of helping us document and make sense of our lives, focused as it is on the next photo rather than the overall story. None of us takes enough time to stop and ponder the larger arc of existence; how could the internet help us do that?

Fourth, the online world should bring together communities of differing ideas, faiths, purposes, and meanings rather than fragmenting them further. We need more forums, not fewer. We need to create more trust, not less. We need to find more common ground, not more hate. How could the virtual world help in this way?

Fifth and finally, the virtual world should help us think longer term rather than shorter term. One of the well-documented effects of our harried virtual lives, with our mobile phones turned on 24-7, is that we have become grazers rather than real consumers of bigger ideas, slower-moving organizations, and deeper connections. How could our superficial, fast, and furious internet give us more profound, well-paced, and joyous experiences?

My journey into the online world to understand the virtual communicator has led me to understand how profoundly inhuman many ways of virtual communication are. The virtual world bleaches out human emotion, when it is emotion that fundamentally allows us to see patterns, create meanings, and form memories. The virtual world takes away one of the deep joys of human interaction—that sense of near simultaneity, when you and I are in sync, communicating effortlessly, immediately, and passionately with hardly any sense at all of the distance between us. And the virtual world substitutes clumsy, colorless, and clownish forms of communication, depriving us of the natural ways in which humans evolved over the millennia to talk to one another without distance, without division, and without despair.

Our very human job now is to learn to put the emotional and the memorable back into this attenuated world that has sprung up around us, the digital dragon's teeth we have sown and that have brought us virtual convenience and speed—at far too high a price.

NOTES

Introduction

1. Piercarlo Valdesolo, "Scientists Study Nomophobia—Fear of Being without a Mobile Phone," *Scientific American*, February 2016.

2. Moira Burke, Cameron Marlow, and Thomas Lento, "Social Network Activity and Social Well-Being," in *Proceedings of the SIGCHI Conference on Human Factors in Computing Systems* [Atlanta, April 10–15, 2010], ed. Elizabeth Mynatt et al. (New York: Association for Computing Machinery, 2010), 1909–1912.

3. Denis Campbell, "Facebook and Twitter 'Harm Young People's Mental Health,'" *Guardian*, May 19, 2017. See also Tara Bahrampour, "Teens Who Spend Less Time in Front of Screens Are Happier—Up to a Point, New Research Shows," *Washington Post*, January 22, 2018.

4. Vanessa K. Bohns, "A Face-to-Face Request Is 34 Times More Successful Than an Email," *Harvard Business Review*, April 11, 2017.

5. Keld Jensen, "People Lie More Often by Email Than Face-to-Face," *Forbes*, July 23, 2014.

6. Christopher Bergland, "Face-to-Face Social Contact Reduces Risk of Depression," *Psychology Today*, October 5, 2015.

7. Nicholas Epley et al., "Egocentrism over Email: Can We Communicate As Well As We Think?," *Journal of Personality and Social Psychology* 89, no. 6 (2006): 925–936.

8. Melinda Wenner Moyer, "Eye Contact Quells Online Hostility," *Scientific American*, September 1, 2012.

9. Adrian Furnham, "The Secrets of Eye Contact, Revealed," *Psychology Today*, December 10, 2014; Michael Argyle and Janet Dean, "Eye Contact, Distance, and Affiliation," *Sociometry* 28, no. 3 (1965): 289–304.

10. Robin Reilly, "Five Ways to Improve Employee Engagement Now," *Gallup Business Journal*, January 7, 2014; Jacques Bughin and Michael Chui, "Evolution of the Networked Enterprise: McKinsey Global Survey Results," McKinsey & Company, March 2013, www.mckinsey.com/business-functions/digital-mckinsey/our-insights/evolution-of-the-networked-enterprise-mckinsey-global-survey-results.

11. Lynn Wu, "Social Network Effects on Productivity and Job Security: Evidence from the Adoption of a Social Networking Tool," *Information System Research*, November 1, 2012.

12. Derek Thompson, "Study: Nobody Is Paying Attention on Your Conference Call," *Atlantic*, August 21, 2014.

13. John Cloud, "Study: Doodling Helps You Pay Attention," *Time*, February 26, 2009.

14. Innocent Chiluwa et al., "Texting and Relationship: Examining Discourse Strategies in Negotiating and Sustaining Relationships Using Mobile Phones," *Covenant Journal of Language Studies* 3, no. 2 (2015): 15–38.

15. Suzanne Wu, "Was It Smart to Use Your Phone at That Meeting?" *USC [University of Southern California] News*, October 24, 2013.

16. Epley et al., "Egocentrism over Email."

17. John Medina, phone interview with the author, August 21, 2017. See also John Medina, *Brain Rules: 12 Principles for Surviving and Thriving at Work, Home, and School*, 2nd ed. (Seattle: Pear Press, 2014).

18. John Medina, phone interview with the author, August 21, 2017.

19. John Medina, "The Performance Envelope," *Brain Rules* (blog), September 25, 2014, http://brainrules.blogspot.com/2014/09/the-performance-envelope.html.

20. Medina, *Brain Rules: 12 Principles*, ch. 4.

21. Nick Morgan, *Power Cues: The Subtle Science of Leading Groups, Persuading Others, and Maximizing Your Personal Impact* (Boston: Harvard Business Review Press, 2014).

22. Annamarie Mann and Jim Harter, "The Worldwide Employee Engagement Crisis," *Gallup Business Journal*, January 7, 2016.

23. Alan R. Teo et al., "Does Mode of Contact with Different Types of Social Relationships Predict Depression in Older Adults? Evidence from a Nationally Representative Survey," *Journal of the American Geriatrics Society*, October 6, 2015. See also Kim Jung-Hyun, Seo Mihye, and David Prabu, "Alleviating Depression Only to Become Problematic Mobile Phone Users: Can Face-to-Face Communication Be the Antidote?," *Computers in Human Behavior* 51, part A (October 2015): 440–447.

24. Morgan, *Power Cues*, here and for the discussion of voice in the remainder of this chapter.

25. A. K. Pradeep, *The Buying Brain: Secrets for Selling to the Subconscious Mind* (Hoboken, NJ: Wiley, 2010), 4.

26. Stanford Gregory, phone interview with the author, April 2012.

Chapter One

1. See, for example, A. D. Craig, "Interoception: The Sense of the Physiological Condition of the Body," *Current Opinion in Neurobiology* 13, no. 4 (2003): 500–505. See also Barnaby D. Dunn et al., "Listening to Your Heart: How Interoception Shapes Emotion Experience and Intuitive Decision Making," *Psychological Science* 21, no. 12 (2010): 1835–1844; Jonathan W. Ho et al., "Bidirectional Modulation of Recognition Memory," *Journal of Neuroscience* 35, no. 39 (2015): 13,323–13,335; Lisa Kinnavane et al., "Detecting and Discriminating Novel Objects: The Impact of Perirhinal Cortex Disconnection on Hippocampal Activity Patterns," *Hippocampus* 26, no. 11 (2016): 1393–1413; S. Takami, "Recent Progress in the Neurobiology of the Vomeronasal Organ," *Microscopy Research and Technique* 58, no. 3 (2002): 228–250.

2. Giacomo Rizzolatti and Corrado Sinigaglia, *Mirrors in the Brain: How Our Minds Share Actions and Emotions*, trans. Frances Anderson (New York: Oxford University Press, 2008).

3. Nick Morgan, *Power Cues: The Subtle Science of Leading Groups, Persuading Others, and Maximizing Your Personal Impact* (Boston: Harvard Business Review Press, 2014).

4. Tim Elmore, "Nomophobia: A Rising Trend in Students," *Psychology Today*, September 18, 2014, https://www.psychologytoday.com/us/blog/ artificial-maturity/201409/nomophobia-rising-trend-in-students.

5. Piercarlo Valdesolo, "Scientists Study Nomophobia—Fear of Being without a Mobile Phone," *Scientific American*, February 2016.

6. Caglar Yildirim, "Exploring the Dimensions of Nomophobia: Developing and Validating a Questionnaire Using Mixed Methods Research" (master's thesis, Iowa State University, 2014).

7. Vicky Kung, "Rise of 'Nomophobia': More People Fear Loss of Mobile Contact," CNN, March 7, 2012.

8. Elmore, "Nomophobia: A Rising Trend in Students."

9. NIDA Blog Team, "Teens and 'Nomophobia': Cell Phone Separation Anxiety," *Drugs & Health* (blog), National Institutes of Health, National Institute on Drug Abuse for Teens, December 9, 2015, https://teens.drugabuse.gov/blog/ post/teens-and-nomophobia-cell-phone-separation-anxiety.

Chapter Two

1. Sandy Pentland, "The New Science of Building Great Teams," *Harvard Business Review*, April 2012.

2. Linda Carroll, "Face-to-Face Interaction Acts Like a 'Vitamin' for Depression, Study Suggests," *Today.com*, October 5, 2015.

3. Chen Wang, Rui Zhu, and Todd C. Handy, "Experiencing Haptic Roughness Promotes Empathy," *Journal of Consumer Psychology* 26, no. 3 (July 2016): 350–362.

4. Lawrence E. Williams and John A. Bargh, "Experiencing Physical Warmth Promotes Interpersonal Warmth," *Science*, October 24, 2008: 606–607.

5. Denis Campbell, "Facebook and Twitter 'Harm Young People's Mental Health,'" *Guardian*, May 19, 2017.

6. Nick Morgan, *Give Your Speech, Change the World: How to Move Your Audience to Action* (Boston: Harvard Business Review Press, 2005).

7. Luke J. Chang et al., "A Sensitive and Specific Neural Signature for Picture-Induced Negative Affect," *PLOS Biology* 13, no. 6 (2015): e1002180.

8. Nick Morgan, *Power Cues: The Subtle Science of Leading Groups, Persuading Others, and Maximizing Your Personal Impact* (Boston: Harvard Business Review Press, 2014), ch. 7.

9. Ibid.

10. Ezequiel Morsella et al., "Homing in on Consciousness in the Nervous System: An Action-Based Synthesis," *Behavioral and Brain Sciences* 39 (2016): e168. doi:10.1017/S0140525X15000643.

11. Ibid.

12. Ibid.

Chapter Three

1. European Commission, "Factsheet on the 'Right to Be Forgotten' Ruling," n.d., www.inforights.im/media/1186/cl_eu_commission_factsheet_right_to_be-forgotten.pdf.

2. Chris Palmer, phone interview with the author, August 25, 2017.

3. Chris Palmer, "Personal Mission Statement," *Chris Palmer Online*, personal web page, July 17, 2017, www.chrispalmeronline.com/s/Personal-Mission-Statement-kjlf.doc.

4. Amy J. C. Cuddy, Susan T. Fiske, and Peter Glick, "Warmth and Competence as Universal Dimensions of Social Perception: The Stereotype Content Model and the BIAS Map," in Mark P. Zanna, ed., *Advances in Experimental Social Psychology* 40 (2008): 61–149.

5. Susan Fiske and Chris Malone, *The Human Brand: How We Relate to People, Products, and Companies* (San Francisco: Jossey-Bass, 2013).

6. *Wikipedia*, s.v. "Disappearance of Morgan Nick," updated March 21, 2018, https://en.wikipedia.org/wiki/Disappearance_of_Morgan_Nick.

7. David Meerman Scott, *The New Rules of Marketing and PR: How to Use Social Media, Online Video, Mobile Applications, Blogs, News Releases, and Viral Marketing to Reach Buyers Directly*, 6th ed. (Hoboken, NJ: John Wiley & Sons, 2017).

8. Carmen Simon, phone interview with the author, September 2016.

9. Carmen Simon, *Impossible to Ignore: Creating Memorable Content to Influence Decisions* (New York: McGraw-Hill, 2016).

Chapter Four

1. Eric Jaffe, "Why It's So Hard to Detect Emotion in Email and Texts," *Co.Design*, October 9, 2014, www.fastcodesign.com/3036748/why-its-so-hard-to-detect-emotion-in-emails-and-texts.

2. Nick Morgan, *Trust Me: Four Steps to Authenticity and Charisma* (San Francisco: Jossey-Bass, 2008).

3. Derek Thompson, "Study: Nobody Is Paying Attention on Your Conference Call," *Atlantic*, August 21, 2014.

4. Global Workplace Analytics, "Latest Telecommuting Statistics," updated June 2017, http://globalworkplaceanalytics.com/telecommuting-statistics.

5. Giacomo Rizzolatti and Corrado Sinigaglia, *Mirrors in the Brain: How Our Minds Share Actions and Emotions*, trans. Frances Anderson (New York: Oxford University Press, 2008).

6. Luke Dittrich, "The Brain That Couldn't Remember," *New York Times*, August 3, 2016.

7. Nick Morgan, *Power Cues: The Subtle Science of Leading Groups, Persuading Others, and Maximizing Your Personal Impact* (Boston: Harvard Business Review Press, 2014).

8. Ibid.

9. Stanford Gregory, phone interview with the author, April 16, 2012.

10. Joshua Feast, CEO of Cogito Corporation, phone interview with the author, January 2017.

Chapter Five

1. Jim Harter and Annamarie Mann, "The Right Culture: Not Just About Employee Satisfaction," *Gallup Business Journal*, April 12, 2017.

2. Jacques Bughin and Michael Chui, "Evolution of the Networked Enterprise: McKinsey Global Survey Results," McKinsey & Company,

March 2013, www.mckinsey.com/business-functions/digital-mckinsey/our-insights/evolution-of-the-networked-enterprise-mckinsey-global-survey-results.

3. Lynn Wu, "Social Network Effects on Productivity and Job Security: Evidence from the Adoption of a Social Networking Tool," *Information System Research*, November 1, 2012.

4. Lynn Wu, phone interview with researcher Sarah Morgan, April 2017.

5. Simon Sinek, *Start with Why: How Great Leaders Inspire Everyone to Take Action* (2009; repr., New York: Portfolio, 2011).

6. Robert B. Cialdini, *Influence: The Psychology of Persuasion*, rev. ed. (New York: Harper Business, 2006).

7. Susan Fiske, phone interview with the author, June 2017.

8. Ibid.

Chapter Six

1. Vanessa K. Bohns, "A Face-to-Face Request Is 34 Times More Successful Than an Email," *Harvard Business Review*, April 11, 2017.

2. Nicholas Epley and Justin Kruger, "When What You Type Isn't What They Read: The Perseverance of Stereotypes and Expectancies over E-mail," *Journal of Experimental Psychology* 41, no. 4 (July 2005): 414–422.

3. Huma Qureshi, "You've Got (Offensive) Mail," *Guardian*, July 27, 2009.

4. Rowena Brown, "Email Communication in the Workplace: Investigating the Impact of Email Stressors, Normative Response Pressure, and Stress Appraisals on Employee Adjustment Outcomes" (PhD diss., School of Psychology, University of Queensland, Australia, 2011).

5. Lea Winerman, "E-mails and Egos," *American Psychological Association Monitor on Psychology* 37, no. 2 (February 2006): 16.

6. Nicholas Epley et al., "Egocentrism over Email: Can We Communicate As Well As We Think?," *Journal of Personality and Social Psychology* 89, no. 6 (2006): 925–936.

7. Paul Aurandt, *Paul Harvey's The Rest of the Story* (New York: Bantam, 1984).

8. Maria Wimber et al., "Retrieval Induces Adaptive Forgetting of Competing Memories via Cortical Pattern Suppression," *Nature Neuroscience* 18, no. 4 (April 2015): 582–589.

9. Eugene Kim, "Slack, the Red Hot $3.8 Billion Startup, Has a Hidden Meaning behind Its Name," *Business Insider*, September 27, 2016, www.businessinsider.com/where-did-slack-get-its-name-2016-9.

10. The quotes and observations in this section are from the author's Skype interviews on September 7, 2017, with various Klick Health personnel, including Keith Liu and Yan Fossat.

Chapter Seven

1. Jessica Digium, "Craziest Thing You've Heard on a Conference Call?," *Spiceworks*, March 19, 2015, https://community.spiceworks.com/topic/849475-craziest-thing-you-ve-heard-on-a-conference-call.

2. Ibid.

3. John Medina, *Brain Rules: 12 Principles for Surviving and Thriving at Work, Home, and School*, 2nd ed. (Seattle: Pear Press, 2014).

4. Rob Matheson, "Watch Your Tone: Voice-Analytics Software Helps Customer-Service Reps Build Better Rapport with Customers," *MIT News*, January 20, 2016.

5. Karin Ulbrich, Stefan Klotz, and Josef Settele, "Combining Computer and Real Environment: Experience from Implementing Biodiversity Research in the Classroom," *Proceedings of EDULEARN14 Conference*, July 7–9, 2014, Barcelona, Spain.

6. Shashank Nigam, CEO of SimpliFlying, phone interview with the author, May 15, 2017.

Chapter Eight

1. Pew Research Center, "Mobile Fact Sheet," January 12, 2017, www.pewinternet.org/fact-sheet/mobile/.

2. Tom Rogers, "How to Design Small Decision Making Groups," www.intuitor.com/statistics/SmallGroups.html.

3. R. I. M. Dunbar, "Neocortex Size As a Constraint on Group Size in Primates," *Journal of Human Evolution* 22, no. 6 (1992): 469–493.

4. D. Roland et al., "Will Social Media Make or Break Medical Conferences?," *British Journal of Hospital Medicine* 76, no. 6 (2015): 318–319.

5. David Meerman Scott, cofounder of Signature Tones, phone interview with the author, June 2017.

6. Roger Courville, phone interview with the author, May 2017.

Chapter Nine

1. Robert Kelly, "Robert Kelly BBC World Interview: On South Korea," YouTube, posted by David Waddell, March 10, 2017, www.youtube.com/watch?v=0M7679g1Bew.

2. John Medina, phone interview with the author, August 31, 2017. See also John Medina, *Brain Rules: 12 Principles for Surviving and Thriving at Work, Home, and School*, 2nd ed. (Seattle: Pear Press, 2014).

3. Kathleen L. McGinn and Eric J. Wilson, "How to Negotiate Successfully Online," *Harvard Business Review*, March 2004.

4. Nikki Blacksmith, John C. Willford, and Tara S. Behrend, "Technology in the Employment Interview: A Meta-Analysis and Future Research Agenda," *Personnel Assessment and Decisions* 2, no. 1 (2016): 12–20.

Chapter Ten

1. Moira Burke, Cameron Marlow, and Thomas Lento, "Social Network Activity and Social Well-Being," in *Proceedings of the SIGCHI Conference on Human Factors in Computing Systems* [Atlanta, April 10–15, 2010], ed. Elizabeth Mynatt et al. (New York: Association for Computing Machinery, 2010), 1909–1912.

2. Denis Campbell, "Facebook and Twitter 'Harm Young People's Mental Health,'" *Guardian*, May 19, 2017. See also Tara Bahrampour, "Teens Who Spend Less Time in Front of Screens Are Happier—Up to a Point, New Research Shows," *Washington Post*, January 22, 2018.

3. Barry Levinson, dir. and writer, *Tin Men*, Touchstone Pictures, 1987.

4. Hafeezullah Amin and Aamir S. Malik, "Human Memory Retention and Recall Processes: A Review of EEG and fMRI Studies," *Neurosciences* 18, no. 4 (2013): 330–344.

5. Kathy Benjamin, "11 Simple Ways to Improve Your Memory," *Mental Floss*, November 16, 2016.

6. Steven MacDonald, "21 Science-Based Selling Techniques," *SuperOffice*, October 23, 2017.

7. Ryan Estis, phone interview with the author, July 2017.

Conclusion

1. Judith E. Glaser and Richard D. Glaser, "The Neurochemistry of Positive Conversations," *Harvard Business Review*, June 12, 2014.

2. Jeffrey D. Karpicke, "A Powerful Way to Improve Learning and Memory," *Psychological Science Agenda*, June 2016.

3. Ray Sanchez, Natisha Lance, and Eric Levenson, "Woman Sentenced to 15 Months in Texting Suicide Case," *CNN*, August 3, 2017.

4. Michael Krigsman, "HR Millennial Report: 'We Want Transparency, Honesty, and Opportunity'—A Conversation with Two Successful Millennials Reveals Important Advice for Employers," *CXO Talk*, September 26, 2015, www.cxotalk.com/article/hr-millennial-report-we-want-transparency-honesty-opportunity.

5. Kristopher Blom, interview with the author, September 2017.

6. Janet Caldow, "Working Outside the Box: A Study of the Growing Momentum in Telework," *Institute for Electronic Government, IBM Corporation*, January 21, 2009.

INDEX

ACKNOWLEDGMENTS

This book came about because so many audience members asked me about virtual communication when I was trying to talk about body language that I had to listen.

Once again, my long-suffering agent, Esmond Harmsworth, helped shape the arguments herein at early stages. And Jeff Kehoe and Harvard Business Review Press took the book from rough to ready. I am deeply grateful to Jeff for his continuing faith in a book that has labored through several violent rewrites in an effort to capture an ever-changing virtual environment.

Thanks to all my clients, friends, and fellow coaches who have said encouraging things that kept me going when the way ahead seemed obscure and uncertain. Thanks, David, Josh, Rick, Vince, Sally, Susan, Ryan, Brian and Dharmesh, Pascal, Lori, Stephen, Jordan and Ashley, Christine, Tamsen, Mitch, Christopher, Mark, Trine, Matt, Tim, Matthew, Jeff, Steve, and many others.

At the heart of what I do is a family business, and without Nikki, Sarah, and Emma, these ideas would be immeasurably poorer. Thanks also to Holly Smith, whose research and enthusiasm helped at a crucial stage. And thanks particularly to Sarah, who labored with me on the research and the early formulation of the ideas.

Thanks again to the whole international family, for belief, love, and encouragement. Thanks, Emma and Dave, Sarah and Jack, Eric and Julia, Howard and Rita.

Finally, to Nikki, my amazing wife, who manages the remarkable feat of listening with both love and discernment. My love always.

ABOUT THE AUTHOR

NICK MORGAN is one of America's top communication speakers, theorists, and coaches. A passionate teacher, he is committed to helping people find clarity in their thinking and ideas—and then delivering them with panache. He has been commissioned by *Fortune* 50 companies to write for many CEOs and presidents. He has coached people to give congressional testimony, to appear in the media, and to deliver an unforgettable TED Talk. He has worked widely with political and educational leaders. He has spoken, led conferences, and moderated panels at venues around the world. During the last election cycle, he provided expert commentary on the presidential debates for CNN.

Nick's methods, which are well known for challenging conventional thinking, have been published worldwide. His acclaimed book on public speaking, *Working the Room: How to Move People to Action through Audience-Centered Speaking*, was published by Harvard Business Review Press in 2003 and reprinted in paperback in 2005 as *Give Your Speech, Change the World: How to Move Your Audience to Action*. His book on authentic communication, *Trust Me*, was published by Jossey-Bass in January 2009. His book on communication and brain science, *Power Cues: The Subtle Science of Leading Groups, Persuading Others, and Maximizing Your Personal Impact,* was published by Harvard Business Review Press in May 2014.

Nick served as editor of the *Harvard Management Communication Letter* from 1998–2003. He has written hundreds of articles for local and national publications, and appears frequently on radio and TV. Nick is a former fellow at the Center for Public Leadership at the Harvard Kennedy School of Government.

After earning his PhD in literature and rhetoric, Nick spent a number of years teaching Shakespeare and public speaking at the University of Virginia, Lehigh University, and Princeton University. He first started writing speeches for Virginia Governor Charles S. Robb and went on to found his own communications consulting organization, Public Words, in 1997.

Nick attributes his success to his honest and direct approach that challenges even the most confident orators to rethink how they communicate.